Celebrity Tattoos

CASSELL
ILLUSTRATED

A CASSELL BOOK

An Hachette Livre UK Company

First published in the UK 2008 by
Cassell Illustrated, a division of
Octopus Publishing Group Ltd.
2–4 Heron Quays,
London E14 4JP

Text, design and layout © 2008 Octopus Publishing Group Ltd.

Distributed in the U.S. and Canada by Octopus Books USA:
℅ Hachette Book Group USA
237 Park Avenue
New York NY 10017

A CIP catalogue record for this book is available from the
British Library.

ISBN-13: 978-1-84403-661-5

10 9 8 7 6 5 4 3 2 1

Editor: Jo Wilson
Production: Caroline Alberti
Creative Director: Geoff Fennell
Publisher: Mathew Clayton

Printed in China

Contents

14 Animals

24 Bikers and Criminals

28 Captain Cook

30 Cape Fear

32 Celtic style

46 Flowers

54 Japanese style

70 Mechanized tatts

72 Memento

74 Miami Ink

86 Prison Break

96 Sailor Jerry

102 Spiritual

104 Suicide Girls

106 Symbols

112 Tribal style

114 20th Century

126 Index

128 Temporary tattoo
instructions

A 10 Christina Aguilera, Pamela Anderson, Billy Joe Armstrong, **B** 18 Drew Barrymore, David Beckham, Travis Barker, David Blaine **C** 34 Cher **D** 36 Johnny Depp, Pete Doherty **E** 40 Eminem **F** 42 Colin Farrell, Flea **G** 48 Sarah Michelle Gellar, Boy George **H** 52 Josh Homme **I J** 56 Angelina Jolie **K** 58 Anthony Kiedis, Johnny Knoxville **L** 62 Tommy Lee, Lindsay Lohan, Courtney Love **M** 68 Marilyn Manson, Alyssa Milano **N** 78 Dave Navarro **O** 80 Ozzy Osbourne **P** 82 Pink, Brad Pitt **Q R** 88 Christina Ricci, Nicole Richie, Dennis Rodman, Henry Rollins **S** 98 Nikki Sixx, Britney Spears, **T** 108 Billy Bob Thornton, Justin Timberlake **U V W** 116 Mark Wahlberg, Pharrell Williams, Robbie Williams, Amy Winehouse **X Y Z** 124 Rob Zombie

Introduction

In recent years tattoo art has become increasingly popular all around the world. Once the preserve of outsiders, sailors, criminals, and theatrical performers, you are now just as likely to find a "tat" on the shoulder of a school-teacher, an accountant, or even your local shopkeeper.

That is not to say that tattoos on men and women are a new development. For as long as mankind has lived together in society he has tattooed himself to indicate membership of a tribe, as a right of passage to adulthood or to commemorate the events and experiences of his lives. Cave paintings, ancient Egyptian hieroglyphs and Celtic stone carvings have all shown that our ancestors used tattoos to beautify the body, to draw on protective forces or to invoke the powers of the divine.

Thanks to its suppression by Judaism, Christianity, and Islam, the practice of tattooing was dormant in the West for over a thousand years. In the modern era, it would be intrepid global explorers who eventually would re-ignite the interest of Europe and America in body decoration as they rediscovered the ancient art among Polynesian tribes and Native Indians of the Americas.

Though the numbers of those wearing tattoos has grown steadily over the past hundred and fifty years, their huge popularity today must be in part attributed to the many high profile celebrity aficionados of the needle from the worlds of film, music, and television. Where would Johnny Depp, Angelina Jolie, P!nk or Drew Barrymore be without their body art? Even less alternative stars like Jessica Alba, Sarah Michelle Gellar, and Anna Kournikova have all chosen to "get inked" to commemorate a pivotal event or a special person in their lives. It's safe to say that tattoos have become as much part of life on the red carpet as designer clothes, limousines and the flash bulbs of the paparazzi.

In the course of this book we'll take a look at the history of tattooing and the diverse artistic and spiritual styles that have developed within the art. We'll also take a closer look at the various pieces of tattoo work that the world's biggest stars have chosen to have etched on their bodies. Many of these tattoos, from David Blaine's piercing eyes to David Beckham's distinctive angels, have unique and personal stories behind them.

Christina Aguilera's cryptic Hebrew lettering and the message over Johnny Knoxville's heart are tributes to loved ones while pieces such as Amy Winehouse's busty woman or the swirling tribal pattern on Robbie Williams' shoulder are both nods to distinctive styles from tattooing's history. The colorful and ornate Japanese hikae found on Nikki Sixx or Colin Farrell's Irish Celtic cross showcase tattoo styles from around the world, while the crazy, self-created designs found on Marilyn Manson, Eminem, and Rob Zombie are striking pieces of original art conceived with the aid of a trusted tattoo artist.

From the jungles of Borneo to the catwalks of Paris, tattooing holds a unique position in our shared culture and remains the ultimate expression of creativity and individuality. Here we have brought together a huge collection of different styles, symbols, and designs from the world of tattooing which range from the comic to the bizarre and from the beautiful to the brutal.

However when it comes to getting inked celebrities make the same decision that any Average Joe or Jane would when they sit in the tattoo artist's chair. What will this permanent piece of body art mean to me? If you are thinking of getting a tattoo, or adding even more work to the pieces you already have, we hope this book will provide you with a little inky inspiration.

Christina Aguilera

Singer Christina Aguilera could be seen as the archetypal good girl gone bad. The former *Mickey Mouse Club* presenter turned music megastar shocked the world when her *Stripped* album went multi-platinum in 2002. Along with *Stripped* came a whole new look for the diminutive singer featuring hair extensions, a raunchy wardrobe, and multiple tattoos.

"People like to see singers play it safe and it scares people if we go beyond the boundaries sometimes", said Christina of her transformation.

The half Ecuadorian pop star has **'Xtina'** prominently tattooed on the back of her neck, a **small flower** on her left wrist as well as well as a Hebrew message **'I am my beloved's and my beloved is mine'** on her lower back and a further tattoo just below her bikini line.

Along with her wild fashion style and her four octave vocal range, Christina is also a devotee of body piercing. Since her marriage she has removed many of her piercings, however over the years she's had many, including her left nostril, a labret in her bottom lip, her right nipple and, reputedly, several genital piercings.

But it is Christina's tattoo on the inside of her left forearm that presents something of a challenge for any budding linguist. This unique tattoo reads **'Te Amo Siempre'** meaning "I love you always" in Spanish surrounded by two distinctive Hebrew letters. The unusual digits read **'Yud'** (Y) and **'Bet'** (B). The combination would be a mystery if you didn't know that the Hebrew alphabet has no letter J and that "Yud" is often used as a replacement. The tattoo therefore actually reads **'JB'**, the initials of Christina's husband, the music mogul Jordan Bratman.

Pamela Anderson
Pamela
Pamela M

Pamela Anderson

Pamela Anderson is the original *Baywatch* babe, *Playboy* centerfold and tabloid superstar. More recently she's been better known as a working mum and PETA activist.

Among Pammy's many groundbreaking contributions is her popularization of tattoo art. She almost single-handedly put armbands on the tattoo map when she had her barbed wire band inked for a film role of the same name. The tattoo became so instantly famous it was arguably responsible for the huge rise in popularity of the tattoo armband throughout the late nineties.

As well as the infamous armband, Pammy has **'Mommy'** on her finger. It used to say **'Tommy'** and served as a permanent wedding band to commemorate her impromptu union with Mötley Crüe drummer Tommy Lee. But after their divorce she changed the piece to reflect her love for the couple's two children instead.

Pammy thinks the kids, by the way, are unlikely to follow their parents into the tattoo parlor. "I don't think they think much of it. We have so many friends that are covered in tattoos, I don't think they'll have to rebel and get a tattoo."

It's this kind of sassy good-humored approach to life that makes us love Pammy. For all her blond ambition the lady and her tattoos are a class act; even if she did accuse Tommy of giving her Hepatitis C when they shared the same tattoo needle.

Pamela has two other notable pieces; a small image on her ankle, and a thin tribal design that runs from the small of her back along her spine.

Pammy says of her tattoos: "Tattoos are like stories; they're symbolic of the important moments in your life. Sitting down, talking about where you got each tattoo and what it symbolizes, is really beautiful."

Animals

– What do they mean?

Animals and birds feature prominently in the tattoo art of nearly all cultures. Sometimes the designs are purely decorative but often they are associated with the strength and beauty of the animal itself. Some of the most popular are:-

Bear – The bear is both feared and admired for its strength. Bear traits include the protection of cubs by females and the belief in bears as spirit guides by shaman.

Bluebirds & swifts – Bluebirds and swifts are nautical tattoos. After a long journey at sea, the sighting of land birds heralded a safe return to port for sailors and so were seen as good luck; sailors who logged 5,000 miles at sea were traditionally entitled to ink on a bluebird in celebration.

Bull – A profoundly macho tattoo, the bull is a symbol of power, strength and fertility as well the star sign Taurus.

Butterfly – Hugely popular with women, the butterfly's short life and delicate breathtaking beauty have made it synonymous with youth and femininity.

Cat – Both domesticated and worshipped by the ancient Egyptians, the cat remains a symbol of independence and free thinking.

Dolphin – Popular with women because of their association with freedom of spirit, dolphins were once thought to rescue drowning sailors. This legend demonstrates the long standing empathy between humans and these magical creatures.

Dove – The dove was associated with the living Holy Spirit by early Christians but, in a wider context, it is a symbol of peace.

Dragonfly – The dragonfly represents the power of light. Inhabiting both air and water, it can pass the power of both elements to the wearer.

Koi, or Carp – Both fish are popular in Japanese tattooing. Koi represent perseverance in the face of adversity and strength of character. The Carp represents wisdom and longevity.

Ladybirds – Tiny, bright red and spotty, ladybirds are always a symbol of good luck.

Lion – The Lion is an ancient symbol which is almost universally recognized as a sign of strength, dignity and wisdom as well as the star sign Leo.

Lizard – Some lizards are able to drop their tails to escape danger, a symbol of guile and self-protection.

Peacocks – Known as "the bird of 100 eyes", the peacock represents an all-seeing witness to the hidden sins of others.

Snake – Embraced by both Eastern and Western tattoo art, the snake is a symbol of wisdom as well as charm and free thought.

Wolf – The wolf is a powerful figure in western folk law. At times ferocious and cruel, the wolf can also be loyal and courageous when defending its pack.

Billie Joe Armstrong

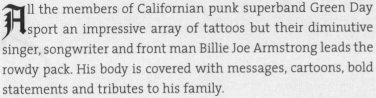

All the members of Californian punk superband Green Day sport an impressive array of tattoos but their diminutive singer, songwriter and front man Billie Joe Armstrong leads the rowdy pack. His body is covered with messages, cartoons, bold statements and tributes to his family.

On his left arm Billie Joe had a **baby smoking a cigar**, a **clown bracelet** showing two clowns holding hands and **E.B.P.M.** (East Bay Punk Mafia) with a **star** on each side of it as a tribute to his musical roots. He also has a **tiger** crawling and a small galaxy of **multi-colored stars**. Further down his arm is **'Jakob'** his son's name, in block letters above a **soccer ball** with **stars,** and **rockets** around it.

His left arm bears another punk tribute, a **circled 27**, the band logo of The Riverdales. On his right shoulder there is a **face** along with **'Adrienne'**, (his wife's name), a **vine**, and two distinctive angels facing each other in prayer. Other messages on this arm include **'All Ages'** written with a star on each side, the Japanese symbols for **pot** and **'pinhead'** written in Katakana (the alphabet used by the Japanese to write English) and his other son's name **'Joseph'** next to a **rose**. On his lower arm he has a **photostrip** of his wife, Adrienne.

On his body Billie Joe expresses his love of classic cars with an **auto** on his chest next to a symbol meaning **'potent male'**. He also has the number 80 on the left side, as well as a **skull** and the word **'PUNX'** on his torso.

Billie Joe's attitude to tattooing is like his music. It shows his chaotic punk roots but remains full on, tongue in cheek but with a serious emotional core. As Billie Joe once said of Green Day: "We put the fun back in dysfunctional."

Drew Barrymore

"**S**ometimes I bust out and do things so permanent. Like tattoos and marriage" said Drew Barrymore of her tattoos. The former wild child star turned Hollywood big hitter has a checkered history of both. As well as a much publicized childhood partying, she has been married unsuccessfully twice – once to bar owner Jeremy Thomas and once to the comedian Tom Green.

While Drew may have been unlucky in love, her forays into body art have been considerably more successful. Drew's tattoos say a good deal about her essentially free-thinking nature and reveal an unexpected interest in the divine.

As Drew has grown older, she has demonstrated a more serious edge to her personality with a series of religiously inspired pieces. She has a large dark **orthodox cross** on her right leg which is wrapped in an **ornate vine**.

Drew's first tattoos were feminine, fun and full of hippie chic. On her belly Drew expressed her flower child side with a colorful **butterfly** under her navel. As Drew called her production company Flower Films, it comes as no surprise that she also chose to add a modest **floral design** on her inside left hip bone just below the bikini line.

However her largest single piece of work is found on her back. Here Drew has added three **guardian angels** at the base of her spine. The first to arrive was a cute looking **cherub** in the small of her back bearing a scroll reading **'Jaid'** (her mother's name). Recently this celestial guardian has been flanked by two equally well conceived helpers both carrying a hefty looking cross.

The final piece in Drew's tattoo portfolio is a tiny, hugely personal addition that shows her fun-loving side; a thumbnail size **blue moon** with a **smile** and a **star** on the big toe of her right foot.

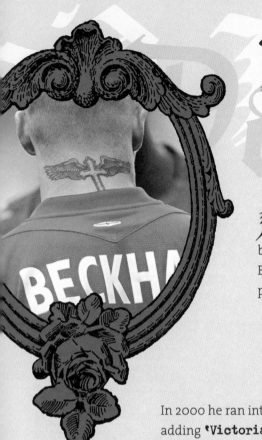

David Beckham

Millionaire soccer star David Beckham is known as much for his love of tattoos as he is for his ability on the football field. He made his name with Manchester United and England, but then took his boots and his fame international, playing for Real Madrid and latterly the LA Galaxy.

Beckham's first tattoo was the name of his son **'Brooklyn'** in Gothic script on his back. This was quickly followed with an **angel** beneath it and he has since added the names of his two other sons **'Romeo'** and **'Cruz'**.

In 2000 he ran into controversy when he paid tribute to his wife by adding **'Victoria'** to his left arm. David had the name inked on in Hindi because he thought English would be "tacky" but some scholars argued the lettering was wrongly spelt (Beckham's script added an "h" to read Vihctoria).

On his underside right arm David has the Roman numeral **VII** (7 was his Manchester United jersey number) which sparked a series of Roman additions; the Latin phrase **'Perfectio In Spiritu'** meaning "Spiritual Perfection" on his right arm and **'Ut Amem Et Foveam'** or "So That I Love And Cherish", on his left.

In 2004 his body art once again caused controversy when he took to the field in the World Cup with a shaved head and a **winged cross** on the back of his neck. Some fans complained the new tat made him look like a hooligan. David's reply was to add another angel with **'In The Face of Adversity'** on his right arm.

Since then he has had the classical art design on his right shoulder expanded with another angel and clouds, and a stunning full body portrait of his wife underscored with **'Forever by your side'**.

As David's stellar career has progressed his body art has become more philosophical. In 2008 he added Chinese characters during a visit to Hong Kong which read **'Death and life have determined appointments. Riches and honor depend on heaven'**.

Travis Barker

Drummer Travis Barker is something of a renaissance man. Along with the multi-platinum-selling band Blink 182, Travis has played in many groups, as well as starting a clothing line, a record label and even a fish restaurant. Most recently he's starred in *Meet the Barkers*, a reality show documenting the ups and downs of his marriage to former Miss USA Shanna Moakler. Along the way Travis has spent an estimated $30,000 creating a full body suit of tattoo art.

Travis got his first tattoo when he was 17, his childhood nickname **'Bones'**. Since then many of his tattoos have documented elements of his life. His humble roots in Fontana, California led to the addition of **'Self Made'** across his knuckles. He also displays a lot of religious art, a portrait of **Jesus** above his left biceps, **hands in prayer** on the left side of his head (along with his signature Mohawk haircut), a **Virgin Mary** dedicated to his mother on one arm and a **sacred heart**.

But religion comes second to his love for Cadillacs. He has **racing flags** on his neck with the number **66**, as well as the classic Cadillac emblem and a **pair of spark plugs** on his chest. He also has the word **'Cadillac'** on the side of his body.

Travis has **'Can I Say'** across his collar bones along with a **microphone** and **beat box** on his stomach all inspired by his love of hip hop. Music also inspired the **Descendents logo** on his left leg as well as the title of their album **'Hope'** which he added to his back after his mother's death.

Tributes to his family include **'familia'** on his arm, **Japanese flowers** with a **heart** that says **'Mom'**, and a heart with **'Shanna'** on its banner. His son's name **'Landon'** is on his left wrist.

Luck also plays a huge part in Travis' tattoos. Gathered on his right arm are a **deck of cards**, **dice**, a **dollar sign**, his lucky number **seven**, a **rabbit's foot**, a **skull** with the number **13**; which is considered lucky by tattoo artists.

In explanation of his large number of tattoos Travis has said, "I tattooed my body so I couldn't fall back on anything. I purposely did that so I couldn't get a normal job and live a normal life. I did it so I had to play music."

Bikers and criminals

Tattoos are now worn proudly by men and women of all ages. In fact an accountant or your kid's school teacher is just as likely to have some ink under their shirt as the local garage mechanic. But this was not always so, the prohibition of tattooing by religious groups, social mores, or even government ban has meant that tattooing has often been seen as the mark of society's outsiders. For years, tattoos were created and worn by those who broke the rules, carved with handmade equipment, and colored with improvised inks by bikers and criminals around the world.

Biker tattoos are usually found on the bicep or forearm, not least as protective motorcycle gear would cover everything else. Largely they're tribal and proclaim the wearer's allegiance to a specific motorcycle gang or organization. Usually you'll find **bikes, flames, snakes, eagles, skulls** and powerful messages of freedom as well as biker gang colors or patches. You'll also find the Harley Davidson name or logo is enduringly popular, sometimes on its own, and sometimes as part of an intricate design.

The most famous of all criminal tattoos are those worn by the Japanese mafia, the Yakuza. The Yakuza favour intricate and traditional designs in a full body suit which can be hidden entirely from view by clothing (and the eyes of the law) as an inescapable sign of commitment to their gang.

Prisons are also hot beds of tattoo art, and none are more sophisticated than Russian prison tattoos. The Russian prison population is one of the largest in the world. From the mid-1960's to the 1980's, thirty-five million people were incarcerated, and of those, it is estimated that twenty to thirty million were tattooed. Recently films such as David Cronenberg's *Eastern Promises* have brought this extraordinary tattooing tradition to public attention. These breathtaking body tattoos are extremely figurative and symbolic, giving explicit details of gang membership, crimes committed and places of incarceration. Look out for military style **epaulets, monasteries** and **cathedrals, Cyrillic characters, spider's webs, stars, kittens, crowns, saints** and **birds.**

Across the world even the smallest of tattoos can have huge significance to the prison population. In the UK a single dot on the cheek indicates the wearer as a "borstal boy", while three dots between the thumb and forefinger proves gang membership among the Latino population of US prisons; more menacingly a teardrop by the eye indicates the inmate is someone who has killed.

David Blaine

David Blaine

Originally coming to fame by plying his trade as a street magician, David Blaine seized the attention of the world with a series of sense-defying illusions in New York and London. In his career Blaine has been frozen in ice, buried alive, perched on a pole and spent weeks in a glass box. Throughout it all he has maintained an air of mystery and personal intensity that is reflected in the tattoos that cover his body,

Perhaps his most instantly recognizable piece is a large tattoo on his right shoulder, an exotic tribal design that frames a picture of his **mother's eyes**. His left shoulder has a **fantasy piece** based around a **face**. He also has a full back piece featuring the famous painting by Salvador Dali **'Christ Of Saint John'**. David has made many small symbolic additions over the years. He has had messages such as **'My Brother'** on his chest and **'God, Faith, Will, Water'** tattooed on his wrist. He also has the writer Primo Levi's concentration camp number, **174517**, tattooed on his left forearm after reading the Jewish author's Holocaust memoir *Survival in Auschwitz*.

David used to have a **'J'** for Josie, his ex-girlfriend, tattooed on his chest but changed it to **'Lonneke'** (the name of another girlfriend) when they split.

Other tattoos include an angel located at the top left hand side of his chest and a mysterious hooded figure on the right hand side of his waist.

As well as his permanent tattoos, David has been known to make others appear as if by magic. Notably **playing cards** or **numbers** chosen by his audience during the course of a trick and the now infamous **'hunger'** tattoo which appeared on the inside of his lower lip during his glass box stunt 'Above the Below'.

Captain Cook
– History part one

Tattooing has existed in many forms around the world since man has walked the earth. However this ancient art was suppressed for nearly two centuries by the rise of Christianity in the West as the result of a prohibition in The Book of Leviticus: "Ye shall not make any cuttings in your flesh for the dead, nor print any marks upon you."

Previously primitive man had always used sticks and sharp stones to adorn his body, scoring his skin and coloring the wound with earth or ashes. It is believed that prehistoric man created such tribal markings to call on divine forces, often visualized through images of animals or birds.

Such totem animals were a common theme in early tattooing. **Snakes, bears,** and **wolves** were all inked in the hope that the wearer might inherit some of their physical attributes or bond with it as a spirit guide. Young men would be tattooed as a rite of passage, not just to brand them to their clan but also to prove their valor should it ever be called upon in battle.

The Ancient Egyptians believed that, as the spirit after death would resemble the human body, tattoos could help a man's soul pass into the spirit world; while the leaders of Celtic tribes tattooed their clan leaders and nobility to demonstrate their social status.

Ancient tattoos were also used to mark the lowest members of society and sometimes administered by force. The Goths used tattoos to identify their slaves while The Romans used tattoos to mark their legionnaires and as a punishment for criminals; carving the crimes, punishments, and even the names of victims into the foreheads of felons.

We owe the revival of tattoos in the West to the native people of Polynesia where the tradition of tribal tattooing had continued without interruption. In New Zealand, Maoris would treat the body like a piece of wood and used bone-cutting tools to carve intricate grooves onto their faces. In Tahiti, tattoos on the body were used to record personal history.

It was in 1769 that Captain Cook first recorded the word "tattoo" to describe the body art of the "savages" he found there. The word itself derives from the Polynesian word 'ta' ("to strike") which describes the sound of a tattooing spike being knocked on skin. Cook's reports caused such a sensation in England that he was dispatched to the islands a second time with the aristocrat Sir Joseph Banks serving as Science Officer.

Cook's crew brought back a fully tattooed Tahitian Chief to the flabbergasted English court. Furthermore both Banks and many of Cook's crew got tattoos themselves sparking interest in the lost art in the highest and lowest levels of society. Overnight these valiant explorers would re-ignite the flame of tattooing across Europe.

Cape Fear

Based on the book *The Executioners* by John D. MacDonald, the seminal psychological thriller *Cape Fear* was rated X for its disturbing content when it was first brought to the screen in 1962. Then it was Robert Mitchum who took the role of vengeful psychopath Max Cady. When Martin Scorsese announced he would remake the film in 1991, few doubted it would result in a landmark performance for his long time collaborator and serial Oscar nominee Robert De Niro as he reprised the role.

De Niro created an entirely new level of menace in his characterization of the convicted rapist turned philosopher, working out how to change his body shape, paying a dentist $5000 to adjust his teeth to make them more "white trash", and covering his torso with a network of crude tattoos that provided a chilling window into the maniac's mind.

The film tells the story of Sam Bowden (Nick Nolte), a small-town lawyer and family-man, who while defending the guilty Cady conceals evidence to allow him to be convicted of a violent rape. Cady spends his 14 year sentence educating himself in philosophy and literature while plotting his revenge on Bowden. On his release, he embarks on an obsessive mission against the man and his family, undermining his career, poisoning the family dog, and brutalizing his daughter Lori. He even comes close to convincing Bowden's wife to sympathize with him. Bowden finds himself caught in a nightmare where he can do little to stop Cady destroying his life. Despite hiring a private detective and appealing to the local Sheriff, he is inevitably drawn towards a final violent confrontation with the sadistic Cady.

De Niro's Cady is a cigar-puffing, scripture-quoting monster. His tattoos were designed for the film to look deliberately rough and ready as if they had been inked in cheap low-class tattoo parlors or by fellow inmates during his long stay in prison. He has a **broken heart** and the word **'Loretta'** on his chest; along his arms he wears dozens of biblical quotations while he has the chilling image of a huge **black cross** from which dangles the scales of justice across his back.

Apart from a single **black panther**, all De Niro's tattoos were technically fakes created for the movie. To his credit De Niro, ever the method actor, did have the grim art tattooed on his body, however he got the tattoo art inked using vegetable dyes that fade after a few months.

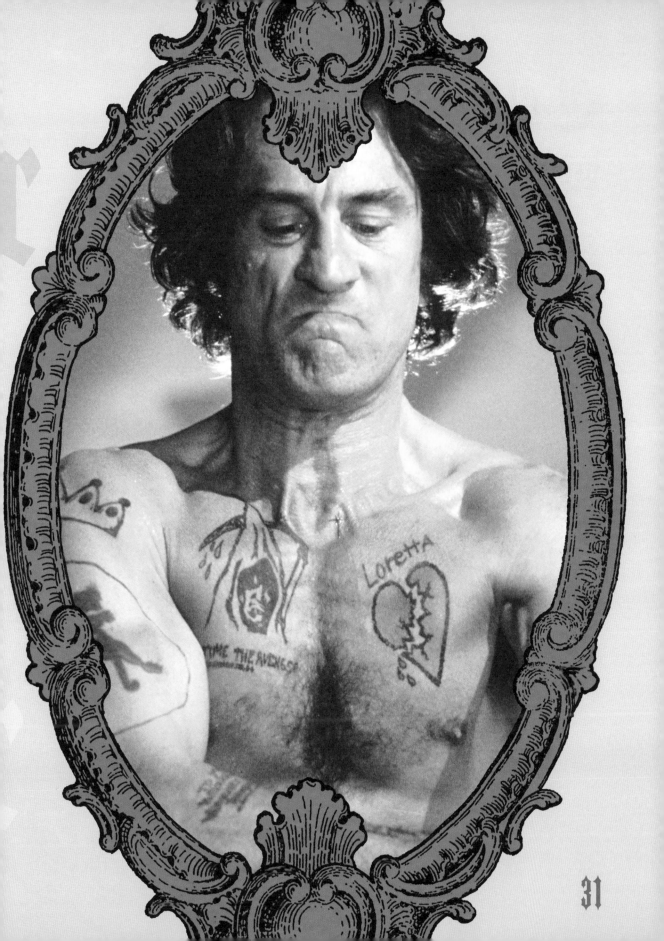

Celtic style

With their intricate and interwoven knot work, strong primitive imagery and complex symbolism, Celtic designs have proved to be enduringly popular with those who seek to get in touch with their Celtic roots.

Though their roots go back to the second century BC, the cultural legacy of The Celts can still be found Scotland, Ireland, The Isle of Man, Wales, Cornwall, and Brittany. Modern Celtic tattoos tend to fall into two categories. Updated re-workings of the ancient body decorations that historians believe were worn by the Celts themselves, and a new breed of modern tattoos which have been inspired by symbols from their culture, such as **beard pullers**, the **claddagh** and **dragons**.

The former are largely based on archeological findings and surviving documents such as the Book of Kells and the Lindisfarne Gospels. Within these ancient manuscripts are found illuminated pages decorated with ornate workings of the letters, patterns and symbols that are now found in armbands and Celtic cross tattoos across the world.

A good example of a Celtic symbol would be the **triquetra**, taken from the Latin "tri quetrus" meaning three-cornered. A **triquetra** is an endless three cornered geometric knot, believed by some to indicate the circle of life and by others to represent the elements of earth, air, and water; though early Christians ultimately co-opted it as a symbol of the Trinity.

The **claddagh** is also popular in body art. This traditional Irish symbol of betrothal consists of two hands holding a heart, topped with a crown. The **claddagh** represents love and commitment but its origins can be traced back four hundred years to a small fishing village in Galway, Ireland.

But perhaps the most recognizable symbol of Celtic culture is its **cross**. Although today it is seen as a decorated symbol of Christian devotion, it also bears the mark of a much earlier Pagan affiliation. Both the cross and the sun-like circle at its centre stood for fertility and agricultural abundance in Pagan lore. While the constantly moving weave that adorns its arms are a symbol of the never-ending cycles of the heavens.

Celtic tattoos offer the wearer a direct link to a lost world of tribal bonds, connection with nature and powerful spirituality. As well as simple beauty they demonstrate a powerful symbolism which can also be found in other popular Celtic tattoos such as **spirals, butterflies** and the **tree of life**. The latter is another design taken from the Book of Kells said to represent "axis mundi", the centre of the world itself.

Cher

Cher is a true superstar. In a career lasting almost forty years, Cher has proved herself to be one of the most popular female performers in history both as one half of Sonny and Cher and as a solo artist. An enduring icon, Cher has sold over 200 million records worldwide as a singer and has won an Academy Award, an Emmy and three Golden Globes as an actress. On top of that she has also found success as a film director, record producer, and author.

Throughout her career, Cher has never been afraid to break boundaries, always embracing new trends and even using plastic surgery to retain her youthful looks. It's easy to forget that Cher became famous for her tattoos, long before they were fashionable among women in Hollywood and she has had a good deal more work done than just a discreet butterfly on the shoulder!

The singer has a **flowing necklace** on her left upper arm with **three charms** hanging on it: an Egyptian **ankh**, the key of life, a **cross** and a **heart**. She also has a **kanji** on her right shoulder (An oriental symbol meaning "power"); as well as a small cluster of Art Deco style **crystals** on her inner right arm.

Cher has a striking **black orchid** design on her right thigh below the bikini line, and another flower, a powerful looking **chrysanthemum**, on her left ankle.

She also has a large **butterfly** and **floral** design created on her buttocks, which was later imitated by androgynous Dead or Alive singer Pete Burns.

In recent years many of Cher's famous tattoos have allegedly begun to disappear and neither the necklace on her left arm nor her Japanese symbol were visible during a recent concert tour. Is it clever make up or the laser? We can be sure Cher will keep us guessing.

Johnny Depp

The tattoos of movie star Johnny Depp say much of his quirky personality and off beat sense of humor. Take for example the **'Winona forever'** banner he had carved onto his arm during his relationship with the actress Winona Ryder. When the couple broke up he decided to forgo the usual laser treatment in favour of creative editing and changed the piece to read **'Wino forever'**.

"My body is a journal in a way." Johnny has said of his tattoos. "It's like what sailors used to do, where every tattoo meant something, a specific time in your life when you make a mark on yourself, whether you do it yourself with a knife or with a professional tattoo artist."

All in all Johnny has thirteen tattoos, many of which signify close family members. He has his daughter's name **'Lily-Rose'** over his heart, his mother's name **'Betty Sue'** in a large heart on his left bicep, and a tribute to his son **'Jack'** on his right bicep underneath a **sparrow** flying over water..

Johnny has been a tattoo aficionado for over two decades, adding new pieces to commemorate significant events in his life. For example the **American Indian** in profile on his right bicep, which is there to represent his Cherokee heritage, or the **skull** on his ankle underlined with the ominous words **'Death is certain'**.

While some of Johnny's tattoos have an obvious meaning, others seem to be as eccentric as the actor himself. He has an inverted triangle on his shoulder and an enigmatic number **3** between his thumb and index finger. While he describes the several small **squares** on his right index finger as little more than a "permanent phone doodle".

Pete Doherty

Singer, songwriter, model, and poet Pete Doherty is a prodigiously talented artist who has arguably found greater fame as a jailbird, drug addict and tabloid bad boy than through his work. Unsurprisingly for someone who takes pride in his skills as a writer Pete's tattoos tell the story of his life and loves in gory detail.

Some of Pete's tattoos are straight down the line old school work. On his lower right arm for example he has a **mermaid** in the classical style. He also has a **skull and cross bones** on his lower right arm that would be more at home on a biker than an effete rock guitarist with artistic pretentions.

However music is never far from Pete's tattoo art. He has **'Libertine'** carved in tribute to his first band across his left arm. His former best friend and band mate Carl Barat also has the same tattoo on his arm. Pete's current band also gets a mention on his body as the singer has **'Babyshambles'** inked around his right nipple.

Across his shoulders he had an extraordinary statement of intent **'Dreams, Romance, Excess'** written in fancy script; a sentiment which "Potty Pete" has done more than most to live out.

However Pete's tattoos also show off the romantic in him. One of his very first tattoos was a **'K'** for an ex girlfriend who he also immortalized in the Libertines song "What Katy did". He has a large **pierced heart** shaped tattoo on his right shoulder in honor of another former girlfriend, the supermodel Kate Moss. On Pete's neck he has the word **'Astile'** which is the name of his daughter by singer Lisa Moorish.

It seems safe to say that despite his recent troubles we haven't heard the last of Pete Doherty nor has he finished adding to the tattoos that mark the progress of his eventful life.

Eminem

The Detroit born rapper, producer and actor has dozens of tattoos across his body. Like his music, each of his pieces serves as a heartfelt confession of his inner turmoil. Just as Eminem expresses his dark side in his alter ego Slim Shady so his body art is sometimes loving and warm but can just as often be dark. Indeed the rapper has one tattoo standing for **Eminem** on one side of his chest, and one tattoo standing for **Slim Shady** on the other side.

On his belly Eminem has a picture of an **open grave** above the message **'Rot in Pieces'**. He had the work done after a fight with his ex wife Kim, assuming he would never get back together with her.

On his lower right and left arms he has the logo of his first band **DI2** in old English script. The **D** on his right arm is also symbolic of the city of his birth, Detroit; the **'I2'** on his left arm completes the piece. On the same arm he also has a **dotted cut line** and **'Slit Here'** on his wrist; while on the other wrist he has a simple tribal band.

On the back of his lower right arm he has an ornate **'Hailie Jade'**, a piece created for his daughter that he had inked on the day she was born. He continues his tribute on his right shoulder where Eminem has a portrait of his daughter, with some roses around her. It also has the words **'Bonnie & Clyde'**, which was a song on **The Slim Shady** LP, and which was also dedicated to her.

On his left shoulder he has created a dark psychedelic fantasy centering around a **magic mushroom** and his Slim Shady persona. Beneath it is a scroll reading **'Ronnie RIP'** in memory of his uncle, Ronnie Pilkington, the man who first introduced him to the hip hop music that would change his life.

Colin Farrell

The tattoos of heart throb actor Colin Farrell say much about the quality of the man behind the celluloid image: passionate and romantic but with a uniquely down to earth view of life.

Though Colin now regularly tops the list of the world's most beautiful people, he came from modest beginnings. Born in CastleKnock, Dublin, Ireland he plied his trade on the small screen before moving to Hollywood and superstardom. "Being Irish is very much a part of who I am. I take it everywhere with me" said Colin. Perhaps it is this strong sense of nationality that is responsible for the wildness of spirit, sense of humour, and search for romance that has dominated the actor's life.

Colin's first tattoo was a **large tribal design** and **arm band** on his left shoulder created in Tahiti during a visit to the islands. Typically off hand he later said of the experience: "Did you ever get a sore in one of your gums above your teeth, where it's sore but you can't stop rubbing it? It's the same kind of thing getting a tattoo. It's sore, but it's kind of nice." Colin's interest in things mystical was further confirmed by a small Buddhist symbol he added inside his right wrist.

However the *Miami Vice* star remains most famous for the tattoos he has inked for love. When he and Amelia Warner exchanged wedding vows, the pair had commemorative tattoos. Colin had his wife's nickname **'Millie'** inked on his ring finger along with the first of two tattoos on his left forearm: a gothic script reading **'Carpe Diem'** (Latin: 'Seize the day') and **'with my girl'**.

The couple's union only lasted four months and following his divorce Colin added a large **Celtic cross** to cover the **'with my girl'**. He did however keep the wedding band. "I'd sooner skip laser treatment and all that and just keep it" he explained. "It's part of me past. But... if I fall in love and it's a problem, or I get married again—God forbid—I'll have a look at getting rid of it." Colin also has a **flower** on his inner arm with a message that reads: **'I love no matter'**.

Flea

Flea, real name Michael Balzary, is the bass player in the rock band Red Hot Chili Peppers. He is known as the driving force behind their success, using his own eclectic taste and off beat style to create the energy that powers his band.

Flea is a man of contradictions. While the Chili Peppers are a uniquely Californian band, Flea was born in Australia. As a musician he plays both aggressive slap bass, as well as more traditional techniques. While he has roots in punk, he loves funk and electronic sounds, and he has appeared on stage with bands as diverse as Nirvana and Jane's Addiction. While being a dedicated and successful musician, he is also an actor who has appeared in such films as *Back to the Future Part II*, *My Own Private Idaho* and *The Big Lebowski*.

Flea has more than half a dozen tattoos. They say a great deal about his love of life and music and give some insight into a more spiritual side to his character.

On his right pectoral, Flea has a Celtic **Triskell** design taken from a burial mound at Ireland. It is supposed to represent the three stages of man: birth, death and eternal life. On his left pectoral he has the name of his daughter's mother, **'Loesha'**.

On his left shoulder Flea has a tattoo of his hero, a huge influence on the Chili Peppers, the guitarist **Jimi Hendrix**. Hendrix tops one of Flea's most distinctive pieces of body art, a colorful ring of a comic book **elephant** walking around his arm. On the underside of the same arm, Flea has an **'X'** that is surrounded by an ornate psychedelic design in tribute to the seminal LA punk band.

On his right bicep, Flea has an impressive looking **snake** tattoo which sits above an **Aztec Bird** tattoo on the underside of his right forearm.

Flea's other tattoos include the word **'Flea'** tattooed on the side of his head and a powerful Aztec style **face** on his back. The latter's brooding energy seems to say it all about Flea. As he once said: "I subconsciously vowed I would somehow create that type of energy to entertain others."

Flowers

- What do they mean?

Flowers are perennially popular in tattoo design all over the world. They can work as an illustrative feature within a larger design, a powerful symbol on their own or just as a pretty picture. Flowers often embody the beauty of nature and its cycles of birth, life, death, and spiritual rebirth.

Cherry – When ripe, this fruit has a strong connection with fertility. However its sweetness means it can also represent chastity and purity.

Chrysanthemum – The word Chrysanthemum comes from the ancient Greek, "chrysos"; meaning gold and "anthemon"; meaning flower. With its full heady bloom it is regarded as the ultimate flower in many cultures. In China it is a symbol of simplicity and perfection. In Japan the "solar flower" is the symbol of the Japanese Royal Family. However some European countries see the chrysanthemum as a flower of death where it is often used in funerals.

Daisy – This flower is derived from "Days eye", because the flower opens at sunrise and closes at sunset. Simple pretty and bright, daisies are associated with the innocence of childhood.

Four-leaf clover and shamrock – Consistently popular with tattoo lovers of Irish descent all over the world, these are both a symbol of hailing from the Emerald Isle and a potent symbol of good luck.

Ivy & vines – Winding vines and creepers have always featured prominently in tattoo art, either combined with floral designs or alone. Vines have long been associated with Bacchus, the Roman god of wine. However Celts regarded the Ivy as a symbol of death and early Christians believed the creeping of ivy towards heaven symbolized resurrection. More recently, Ivy has been associated with fidelity and marital love. On a practical note, Ivy allows a tattoo artist to gracefully integrate different images across the body.

Jasmine – The delicate Jasmine flower is renowned for its evocative and sensual scent. It is the Hindu symbol of love.

Rose – Of all flower tattoo designs, the rose is the most popular. The flower's dramatic beauty, scent and shape mean it is associated with true love. Where the bloom is represented with its thorn, the design warns that its owner, while passionate, should be approached with caution.

Sarah Michelle Gellar

Buffy star Sarah Michelle Gellar was destined for the stage from an early age. Born in New York City, she attended the Professional Children's School where fellow alumni included Melissa Joan Hart, Tara Reid, Jerry O'Connell and Macaulay Culkin. She got her first break in acting at the age of four after being spotted by a talent scout and cast in the 1983 TV movie, *An Invasion of Privacy*. But Sarah would have to wait a few more years before she became a worldwide star in *Buffy The Vampire Slayer*, during which time she took small parts in TV shows and even spent a couple of years as a competitive figure skater.

In 2000 Sarah cemented her position as the queen of the new Hollywood royalty when she married her co-star Freddie Prinze Jr after the couple met and fell in love on the set of teen slasher blockbuster, *I Know What You Did Last Summer*.

Sarah has four tattoos, all of which seem to relate to finding strength and commitment through her marriage. The first is on her right ankle and is the **Tao** symbol for patience, a **heart** and a **dagger**, perhaps to represent the importance of making the most of your relationship. On her left ankle she has a **cherry blossom**, the Chinese symbol for "sincerity". The third, located on her left hip, is a larger Chinese symbol meaning **'integrity'**.

Both Sarah and Freddie share a love of dragons and dragonflies. So it comes as no surprise to find that Sarah's largest tattoo is a pair of **purple dragonflies** in the center of her lower back. The couple both had tattoos done for the first year anniversary, with Freddie inking a matching dragon on his shoulder in honor of his new wife.

Boy George

'DJ and singing star Boy George remains one of the UK's most enduring and colorful musical exports. A key player in the New Romantic movement of the early 1980s, George exposed its high fashion ethic and androgynous experimentation to the international stage when he shot to stardom fronting the pop band Culture Club. Since then his consistent reinvention and outspoken views have meant he's never been far from the headlines.

It seems inevitable that George's tattoos would turn out to be as bold and unusual as the man himself. His most traditional tattoo is a good sized but sparsely designed **cross** on his right shoulder, perhaps created in tribute to his Irish Catholic roots.

However it is on his head that his most striking pieces have been added. The Karma Chameleon star has a **'G'** with tribal design around it on the side of his neck behind his ear and a large **red lotus flower** on the back of his neck to symbolize rebirth and new life.

Though the top of George's head is usually covered with one of his trademark hats, the singer has a large **Star of David** on its crown. It was speculated at the time that the star first appeared that George was considering converting to Kabballah, a fashionable branch of Judaism favoured by celebrities; however George neither confirmed not denied the rumours, probably preferring the speculation.

In recent years George may have become more famous on both sides of the Atlantic for his personal life than his music but his legacy cannot be denied. One thing's for sure, George doesn't add anything to his body without thinking about the impact it will create. When asked the secret of his success he once explained: "I knew style and content went hand in hand."

Josh Homme

Josh Hom Josh Hom Josh Hom

Standing 6'5" tall and topped with flaming red hair, singer and rock guitarist Josh Homme has always been an imposing figure with a clear idea of what he wants and how to get it. He was a founding member of the desert rock band Kyuss, he also founded and remains the only continuous member of the hard rock band Queens of the Stone Age, in which he sings and plays lead guitar and occasionally bass. If that wasn't enough, he co-founded and occasionally performs with the Eagles of Death Metal and produces, performs, and releases material with a diverse array of musicians including Melisa Auf der Maur, Peaches, and the Foo Fighters.

Josh has a series of tough, rough and ready biker-style tattoos on his body. For example, his **grandparent's initials** are tattooed on his knuckles along with a classic **suit of playing cards**.

In reply to fellow bassist Lemmy from Motorhead's **'Born to lose'** tattoo, Josh has the opposite, **'Born to win'**, inked onto his right forearm. The statement is set beneath a **straight razor** to signify that Josh means to take care of business in the most direct way possible. Josh explains his unique philosophy as follows: "The life game goes in both directions, and I don't play the negative way."

But things haven't always gone Josh's way and The Queens of the Stone Age's darkest day has also contributed a tattoo to Josh's collection. Referring to their appearance at the famous Rock am Ring hard rock festival in Germany in 2002, the singer claims it was the "worst show we've ever played and it was in front of 40,000 people". Indeed the band's performance was so bad that after the gig, all its members decided to tattoo themselves with **'Freitag 4.I5'** – the time they started to play – in order to remember it.

Japanese style

The intricacy and beauty of Japanese tattoo art has made it increasingly prevalent in recent years. **Kanji characters, 'Noh' theatre masks, koi and carp, tigers, birds, flowers,** and **Foo dogs** are all popular images represented in a kaleidoscope of patterns and strong colors.

In Japan, the practice of irezumi (which literally means to insert ink under the skin to leave a decorative mark) extends back into the country's early history; though the more elaborate form of tattooing we see today probably has it roots in the Edo period, between 1600 and 1850.

The inspiration for Edo tattoos comes from developments in woodblock printing used to illustrate the era's most popular book, *The Suikoden* (translated as *The Water Margin*). The book told the tale of outlaw heroes, many of whom had their bodies decorated with **dragons, flowers,** and **religious devotions** meant to indicate that the character has taken on the power of the symbol represented. Public fascination with the book led to similar tattoos appearing on the bodies of fans in all sections of society, notably the much respected firemen of Edo. So influential are these original prints that they are being used today as inspiration for tattooists around the world.

Modern Japanese tattooing is often associated with wide body coverage. Again this is thought to have originated from the end of the Edo period where laws concerning conspicuous displays of wealth led the nobility to hide their intricate tattoos beneath their clothing.

Elements of these traditional body suits can be found in today's hikae, or chest panels, that blend work on the shoulders and arms onto the chest. While the upper part of the torso is covered a bare vertical strip of skin is left to run down to the abdomen to creating the effect of an unbuttoned shirt, thought to mimic the line of a samurai's campaign coat.

Tattooing changed radically in Japan at the turn of the century when the Government banned tattoos altogether in order to present a good impression to the visiting Western traders. Soon tattoos became associated with underworld activity, and traditional Japanese tattoos became the preserve of the Japanese mafia, the Yakuza. To this day public baths, health clubs and spas in Japan may still refuse entry to visitors with tattoos.

When considering traditional irezumi, it is worth remembering that it is an art practised by specialist tattooists using ancient techniques. The tattoos are hand tapped with a hammer, bamboo needle and black Nara inks. It is painful, time-consuming and expensive but still an absolutely unique experience.

Angelina Jolie

Actress Angelina Jolie is probably the world's most famous tattoo enthusiast. The daughter of Oscar winning actor Jon Voight describes herself as "still a punk kid with tattoos" but she has received three Golden Globes, two Screen Actors Guild Awards, and an Oscar during her career as well as marrying the actors Jonny Lee Miller and Billy Bob Thornton, becoming the mother to four children and the partner of Brad Pitt.

Angelina has been collecting tattoos since her teens and has thirteen to date. Among these is a Tennessee Williams quote **'A prayer for the wild at heart, kept in cages'**, which she got on her inside left forearm with her mother, an Arabic phrase meaning strength of will, the Latin proverb **'quod me nutrit me destruit'** (what nourishes me destroys me), one of her favourite song titles **'Know your rights'** in gothic script across her neck and a **Yantra prayer** written in the ancient Khmer for her son Maddox on her left shoulder.

Also for her children, she inked four sets of **geographical co-ordinates** on her upper left arm indicating the longitude and latitude of their birthplaces. Other family tattoos include the letter **'H'** for her brother James on her left wrist and the letter **'M'** for her mother Marcheline Bertrand on her hand.

Angelina's tattoos range from the small and discreet like the Chinese symbol for **courage** on her elbow, to the unmissable like the **large cross** on her bikini line, of which she said: "I dropped my pants in a tattoo parlour in Amsterdam. I woke up in a waterbed with this funky-looking dragon with a blue tongue on my hip... I got a cross to cover it. When my pants hang low, it looks like I'm wearing a dagger!" She also has a breathtaking 12-inch **Bengal tiger** on her back which took more than two hours to complete in a Bangkok hotel room.

Over time Angelina has also removed several tattoos, including **'Billy Bob'**, the name of her former husband, which used to sit beneath the dragon on her right arm, a **window** on her lower back and even the first tattoo she ever had – a **Japanese kanji** symbolizing death.

57

Anthony Kiedis

Musician Anthony Kiedis is some time actor and front man for one of the world's famous rock bands, the Red Hot Chili Peppers. Nicknamed "The Swan", Anthony is also known for his bold tribal tattoo work and his long list of celebrity girlfriends, having been linked with Ione Skye, Sofia Coppola, Melanie Chisholm, Sinéad O'Connor, Heidi Klum, and Nina Hagen. Most recently the singer has turned writer and penned a hard-hitting tell-all autobiography dealing with his recovery from drug addiction, *Scar Tissue*.

Anthony has nine tattoos on his upper body. Among his earliest tattoos are the Indian heads found on each of his shoulders. The portraits are of the American Indian Chiefs, **Chief Joseph** and **Sitting Bull**, taken from old photographs. The pair symbolize the singer's Cherokee heritage which he has also immortalized in the Chili Peppers song "Fight like a brave". Beneath each of the chiefs is a bold **tribal armband**.

Also on his right arm, Anthony has an impressive-looking **tiger** that runs from the end of his wrist to his elbow. This is balanced with a **pair of mirrored Celtic serpents** that run along the underside of both of the singer's forearms.

His distinctive tribal back piece of a **totem pole styled eagle** was created at the Museum of Tattoo in Amsterdam by his friend, and legendary tattoo artist, Hank Schiffmacher. Anthony's tattoos are all bold statements that express both strength and sensitivity. One thing is for sure, the ladies love them; a fact that is not lost on the man himself. In fact Anthony set out a clear statement of intent in the Chili's song "Mellowship Slinky in B Major" when he sang: "Can I get another kiss from you? Kiss me right here on my tattoo."

Johnny Knoxville

Philip John Clapp is the real name of Johnny Knoxville the American comic actor and daredevil. Johnny, who took his name from his birthplace in Tennessee, has starred in a number of films, including *Dukes of Hazzard* and *Men in Black 2*, but came to real fame as the co-creator and principal star of the MTV series *Jackass*.

Knoxville fell into his role as *Jackass'* lead protagonist after moving to California to become an actor. Initially he found little success, and appeared only in commercials and as an extra. Eventually he came up with the idea to test self-defence equipment on himself for the skateboarding magazine *Big Brother*. The videos of the fantastically painful and dangerous stunts quickly became a cult favourite around Hollywood and the show was born.

Despite his wild man image Johnny was married to the same woman, Melanie Lynn Cates, for twelve years. They have a daughter **Madison** and Johnny has her name tattooed right over his heart.

Johnny also has a cartoon **hooded face** with prominent teeth on his left bicep above the word, **'Leon'**, which is meant to represent the boxer Leon Spinks. Like much of Johnny's life, the decision to get this tattoo was a spur of the moment thing. Johnny told one interviewer: "I was sitting in a bar, thinking 'I should get a tattoo of Leon Spinks on my arm!'"

As well as his Leon tattoo, Johnny has a lot of small additions. On his left shoulder he has the logo for American punk band The Germs while a banner on his upper right arm reads **'Phil and Lemoyne's Boy'** above the outline of a **bear** that says **'grrrr...'**. He has a circle on the inside of his right hand, and a **lightning bolt** on his left as well as a small tribal design inside his right wrist which he claims really hurt when it was done.

Not that a little pain from a tattoo needle should mean much to the host of show that once saw one of his co-presenters, Steve-O, tattooed in the back of a moving Hum-Vee. As Johnny says: "It's a real primal thing, watching someone get hurt, it's funny and accessible."

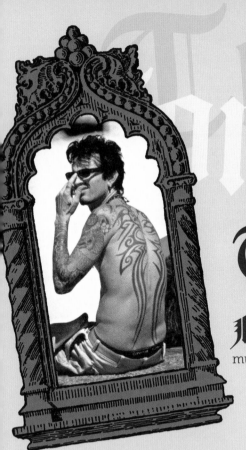

Tommy Lee

Motley Crue drummer turned *Rockstar Supernova* reality TV star Tommy Lee is as famous for his tattoos as he is for his music, run-ins with the paparazzi, and his two celebrity wives. Tommy got his first tattoo in twenties just as the "Crue" began to hit the big time. The tat was of his childhood hero **Mighty Mouse** because as Tommy later explained 'he always gets the girl'.

Since that day the bad boy rocker has become a tattoo addict adding two full sleeves featuring **tigers, koi carp, dragons, flowers,** and assorted other Japanese designs. Across his belly he sports his now infamous **'Mayhem'** tattoo in gothic script which is complimented by nipple piercings. Tommy also wears a full tribal back piece which he has recently had extended over both shoulders and completed with a pair of matching **eagle heads**.

The former Mr Heather Locklear also wears tribal patterns around both ankles and an impressive **raven** on his right thigh. There has been a multiplicity of smaller additions over the years from **stars** on both his hands to a **lipstick kiss** on his neck, though Tommy says that his favorite tattoos are the ones he wears of his two son's names. The boys wrote their signatures on Tommy's wrists then the proud father had the letters inked on.

Like Tommy's life, his love of the needle has had its highs and lows. When Tommy tied the knot with Pamela Anderson, he chose to have his **wedding band** tattooed on his finger but the couple split three years later. While in 1998 the trouble prone rocker sensibly had a tattoo of a swastika removed during a court appearance for affray. On the positive side in 2008 the irrepressible Mr Lee entered tattooing history, and the Guinness Book of Records, when he became the first man to be tattooed in mid air during a private flight to Miami.

Lindsay Lohan

Recently Lindsay Lohan has become more infamous than famous. A regular visitor to rehab facilities, the actress and sometime pop singer is fighting a losing battle with the paparazzi and her hard partying lifestyle.

Lohan started in show business as a child fashion model and had begun acting professionally by the age of ten. At the age of eleven she made her motion picture debut playing identical twins in Disney's 1998 remake of *The Parent Trap* and quickly established herself as one of Hollywood's most bankable young stars with films like *Freaky Friday, Confessions of a Teenage Drama Queen, Mean Girls* and *Herbie: Fully Loaded*. In 2004, Lindsay launched a second career in pop music producing the albums *Speak* and *A Little More Personal*.

Lindsay's first piece of body art was a small tattoo of a **star** on her forearm. Her second tattoo was the Italian phrase **'la bella vita'**, meaning "life is beautiful", in fancy scripting on her lower back. Lindsay intended the tattoo to be a dedication to her Italian grandfather. She also has a tiny white heart tattooed between her thumb and index finger on her left hand.

Lindsay's most infamous tattoo is the word **'breathe'** written in script on the inside of her right wrist. The actress has said the tattoo is a reminder of how important life is after she suffered a dangerous asthma attack in 2005. The words come from John Lennon who said: "Get out there and get peace, think peace, live peace, and breathe peace, and you'll get it as soon as you like."

Such is Lindsay's love of body art that it has been reported that she is planning to open a high end tattoo parlor of her own. Allegedly the star had informed her business partners to begin recruiting tattoo artists with the idea of merchandising the concept. But as yet no such business has opened.

Courtney Love

Rolling Stone once called Courtney Love "the most controversial woman in the history of rock". The American musician and Golden Globe nominated actress is best known as the lead singer, songwriter, and lyricist for the alternative rock band Hole and for her brief marriage to late lead singer of Nirvana, Kurt Cobain, but she has also achieved considerable success as an actress in films such as *The People Versus Larry Flynt* and *The Man in the Moon*.

Throughout her career, Courtney has remained as abrasive and opinionated as the day she first stepped into the limelight. Never afraid to speak her mind or to criticize other celebrities, she has had well publicized run-ins with Dave Grohl, Sharon Osbourne, and the magazine *Vanity Fair* to name but a few. As Courtney says of her chequered past and many feuds: "I found my inner b**** and ran with her".

As a musician Courtney has been at the epicentre of alternative rock for almost two decades, initially hanging out with the likes of The Teardrop Explodes and Echo & the Bunnymen in Liverpool before returning to America and joining the burgeoning Seattle grunge scene that would eventually take the country by storm.

Despite this hard rocking history, Courtney's tattoos are rather restrained and demonstrate a softer more feminine side. Her largest is an Art Deco **angel** on her right shoulder to which she has subsequently added **twin hearts, stars,** and **vines**.

She has a bracelet around her right ankle with **vines,** and **four leaf clovers**. The clovers are for luck however Courtney's nickname is also clover and it is this name she is known to use on internet chat forums.

Her final piece is a small letter **'K'** in the middle of her chest: a poignant and telling symbol of the memory of her late husband which she has promised to "tend every day".

Marilyn Manson

Rock singer Marilyn Manson has long been interested in the manipulation of his persona to create maximum effect on stage and created many of his tattoos before he achieved fame.

Most of his tattoos were created by the staff at Tattoos By Lou in Miami, Florida. Over four years as he climbed the ladder of success Manson worked with Lou's artists to create a unique look that expressed his interest in the gothic horror and the occult.

On his left shoulder Manson has a lucky **red devil** tattoo with crowned horns framed inside a flame-decorated **horse shoe** with a triple-six of tumbling **dice** below. Beneath it sits **Baphomet** the goat of the Sabbath in medieval sorcery. On the right shoulder is a single-horned green **Cyclops head**.

The self-proclaimed "God of F*ck" has a circular green eye at the center of a mass of black tentacles on his inner arms, based on the mythical creature **Cyaegha**. Even Donovan Stringer, the artist who created them, was unclear what they were. He did recall that he charged Manson $50 plus a six pack of beer for the work.

On his forearms, Manson has a pair of **eerie faces**. On the right, is a long and narrow **skull** topped with a **spooky tree** gripping the top created from an original sketch by tattooist Albert Sgambati. On the left he has **Uncle Creepy**, based on the comic book character of the same name.

In recent years Manson has added several smaller items – a green **totenkopf skull** on his upper left arm, a **'Beelzebub'** fly, a **spiral heart** of his own design and a **butterfly** on his wrist. The 'Beelzebub' fly we assume was just in case anyone might forget who they were dealing with. However with Manson's dress sense and these grotesque sleeves, it seems highly unlikely.

Mechanized tats

– History part two

Captain Cook's crew was the first of a new generation of sailors who passed the time during long journeys at sea carving designs into their skin. These seamen picked up new tattoo skills from around the world and collected exotic designs to commemorate their travels; soon **Dragons** from China, **evil eyes** from the Middle East and complex **Edo** designs from Japan all entered the tattoo canon.

Body art also became increasingly popular among the English aristocracy and by the 19th century, tattooing was common place in high society parlors and country houses. Indeed even the great Queen Victoria was said to have had a small tattoo in an "intimate" location.

Her grandson, King George V had himself inked with the **'Cross of Jerusalem'** during a trip to the Middle East and Winston Churchill's mother, Lady Randolph Churchill, had a tattoo of a **snake** around her wrist, which she covered with a diamond bracelet at formal occasions (Churchill himself had an **anchor** on his forearm). By 1898 it was estimated that as many as one in five members of the gentry were tattooed with a **family crest** or a memento of travel or military service.

In America, tattooing was more egalitarian. Tattoos had become popular as a form of basic cosmetic surgery with people adding beauty spots and permanent color to lips and eyes. Such popular tattooing was made possible by mechanization of the process which reduced the time it took to create a piece from hours to a few minutes; allowing tattoos to change from carefully conceived artwork towards stock pieces picked from the walls of the tattoo parlors. Such "tattoo flash" was first made available by a business set up by Charlie Wagner in Chatham Square, New York City. Sailors, criminals and low-lives all flocked to the new parlor, which was conveniently located near the city's red light district.

The modern tattoo gun owes its origin to the electric engraving machine invented by Thomas Edison in 1876. This rotary device was perfected by Samuel O'Reilly who discovered that Edison's machine could be used to introduce ink into the skin, refined the needle system and added a tube to feed ink into a design. However tattoo aficionados will be more familiar with machines powered by electromagnetic coils, the first of which was patented by Thomas Riley in 1891 using a single coil. The faster twin coil machine was created by Alfred Charles South in 1899.

The new machines allowed tattoo artists to control the speed and depth of the needle and to experiment with a range of colors and intricate patterning that offered them almost infinite possibilities in the work they could create.

Memento

Memento is a tense psychological thriller which marked the directorial debut of Christopher Nolan, the man whose dark imagination has since brought us blockbuster hits such as the *The Prestige* and *Batman Begins*. The film is notable for the fact that the action is revealed in short, ten minute segments that move backwards in time. This leaves the audience, and its hero Leonard Shelby (Guy Pearce), desperately trying to piece together events via the network of erratically rendered tattoos that appear across his body.

Leonard is a former insurance investigator who is searching for the man he believes killed his wife during a burglary. His task is not helped by the fact that Leonard is suffering from severe amnesia, which he contracted from a head injury during the attack. From the moment he awakes in a strange hotel room, Leonard is unable to create new memories so he chronicles his investigation via a system of notes to himself, Polaroid photographs (to identify the people he meets and places he goes), and tattoos to record vital information about himself and his task.

The largest of these tattoos (**'John G. Raped and Murdered My Wife'**) gives us the central premise of the plot and is written right across Leonard's chest. Thoughtfully it is added in backwards script so that Leonard can read it in a mirror. Below that – in case we missed it – is **'find him and kill him'**. Scattered across the rest of his body and arms is a collection of important facts, telephone numbers, names, and even car license plates.

Usually Leonard creates these tattoos himself but he sometimes has them professionally applied. In one scene we see Leonard making a mark on his own thigh using a technique known well to school boys the world over – a sewing needle stuck into a ball-point pen dipped in regular pen ink to create a crude tattoo. In another scene, Leonard pulls over his car determined to get one vital fact noted on his body before it is forgotten. This time he drops in on a professional, Emma the Tattooist (Marianne Muellerleile), who adds the license plate number of the man that Leonard is trying to find to his leg.

There's no way one could recommend Leonard's approach to body art to anyone, though their constant presence on his body does serve to help keep the tortured protagonist focussed on his task. One can only hope that he remembers to add a new tat when he finally catches up with his prey or he could be at it forever.

Miami Ink

Miami Ink is a reality TV show that documents the activities of a popular Miami tattoo parlor. In the style of *Ice Road Truckers* and *American Chopper* the show is as much about the daily lives of the staff and their customers as it is about the art of tattooing. Now in its third season in the US, the series is based in a real life tattoo shop "Love Hate Tattoos" in Miami Beach which is rebranded as "Miami Ink" during filming. The shop is owned by straight talking Ami James and his fun loving partner Chris Núñez, both of whom feature in the show. Having grown up in South Beach, Chris and Ami originally became friends while working together at a local tattoo shop. They went on to open their own place and, with a friend of Ami's, put together the idea for *Miami Ink* which they eventually sold to TLC/The Discovery Channel.

Joining Ami and Chris are a host of permanent and visiting tattoo artists who star in the show including elder statesman Chris Garver, the loveable Darren Brass, and their apprentice Yoji Harada, who is frequently the subject of practical jokes by the rest of the crew. Other artists who have appeared include James Hamilton, Luke Wessman, Mikey Slater, J Morgan Pennypacker and Kat Von D. Each episode of the show features a number of customers and explores the stories behind the tattoos they have chosen. The audience stays with customer and artist as each tattoo is created. Along with the customers, each week the audience is invited into the world of the tattoo artists themselves, documenting their ups and downs, the tensions within the shop and following them as they achieve their various dreams and ambitions beyond the shop itself. The show is held together with narration from James and Nuñez as well as colorful montages of the vibrant life of the city of Miami. Celebrity customers of the show have included Bam Margera, Anthony Bourdain, Craig Fergusson and "Fieldy" Arvizu from Korn.

The show has also made celebrities of the staff, not least Kat Von D who, after returning to Los Angeles at the end of the second series, has starred in her own spin off show, *LA Ink*. Another spin-off, *London Ink*, began in the UK in September 2007. Despite the slick graphics and fast cutting on the show, Ami James maintains it is a true portrayal of the life of a tattoo artist: "What a lot of people don't know about me is that I am not playing a character on the show. I am the same person in my real life as I am on TV".

Alyssa Milano

Child star Alyssa Milano began acting at the age of eight. She starred in a host of films before striking it huge in a series of successful TV shows such as *Melrose Place*, *Spin City*, *My Name is Earl*, and of course *Charmed*.

The actress also has a tattoo history as long as her filmography and just as colorful. Her first tattoo was a **fairy** on her hip as a token of her youth. The **rosary beads** on her shoulder are also a part of her childhood. Alyssa was raised on Statten Island New York as part of an Italian Catholic family and the beads are copied from her own rosary collection. Despite the family connection, her parents don't seem too impressed by Alyssa's love of body art: "Every time I get a tattoo, my parents say they'll disown me," she says.

Alyssa also has an **angel** on one ankle and a **vine of flowers** on the other. There's no religious connection here however, the actress simply had them done "because angels and flowers are cool."

Alyssa has a **sacred heart** on her lower back, as a symbol of passion and commitment to life and a **Sanskrit symbol** on the back of her neck. Passion of a different kind is found in the Buddhist symbol of **Om** on her left wrist to remind her of her ex-husband.

Her seventh and most recent tattoo is found on her right wrist. It is an **ourobous** – a snake biting its tail – which is said to be a symbol of rebirth. Alyssa got the reptile inked on after spending time in South Africa after her divorce.

Despite Alyssa being well known in Hollywood for her tattoos, they all have to go when she steps in front of the camera. "I have to get them airbrushed for *Charmed*. Witches don't have tattoos, I guess."

Dave Navarro

Guitarist and rock god Dave Navarro has had an incredible life. His mother was murdered, he played with both Jane's Addiction and the Red Hot Chili Peppers, and he was married to *Baywatch* babe and *Playboy* model Carmen Electra.

Dave has more reasons than most to make a permanent record of his life and has a complex array of tattoos across his body from the obvious to the downright obscure.

Dave has too many pieces to list so here are the highlights. The guitarist has his mother's name ‘Constance’ across his lower back in gothic script and ‘Los Angeles’ the city where he was born on his neck.

On his left arm Dave has a **pig** surrounded by a **snake**, the pig is Dave and the snake the world. He also has a ring of **dolphins** from a trip to Hawaii with the Chili Peppers and two pieces of art; the Gustav Klimt painting ‘Death and Life’ and the ‘Virgin of Guadalupe’ by Mark Mahoneyo. There are also tattoos of **suits of cards** as well as the word ‘addict’.

On his right arm he has a **rose**, inked in tribute to an Auschwitz survivor; the Chili Peppers One Hot Minute fairy logo, a **Sanskrit armband** and the message ‘Love Fades’. There is also a **skull and cross** and more messages ‘Der Zeit Ihre Kunst, Der Kunst Ihre Freiheit’ ("To every age its art, to art its freedom") and ‘Jane's’ in reference to Jane's Addiction. Dave also has the Japanese kanji ‘fuku’ which means fortune and luck. His right arm also bears Dave's personal philosophy in fancy script ‘Trust No One’.

Dave has **bats** on both shoulders and across his collarbone ‘Eleven Twenty-Two’ his wedding date. Beneath that is ‘CE’ (his wife's initials). On his legs he has a **sexy nun** and a **busty female dominatrix**. His elbows both have **Tarot symbols**.

On the hands Dave has birthdays – on his left hand knuckles the Roman numerals **X III X III** his father and grandfather's birthdays, and on his right hand **VI VII VI VII**, his own birth date.

As Dave says "My skin is my canvas. The artwork on it represents something that is very powerful and meaningful in my life. I look at my skin as something of a living diary because all my tattoos represent a time in my life."

Ozzy Osbourne

Before The Osbournes made him an internationally famous reality TV star, John Michael "Ozzy" Osbourne was the lead singer of the heaviest of all metal bands Black Sabbath. Things looked bleak for Ozzy when he was kicked out of the band in 1979 but he went on to become a multi-platinum-award-winning solo artist, found the huge touring rock show Ozzfest and claim his undisputed position as the "Godfather of Heavy Metal"; or as Ozzy prefers "the Prince of f***ing Darkness".

Ozzy has enjoyed a career that has spanned nearly four decades, a miracle when you consider that the wild man of rock has narrowly cheated death several times. Along the way he has collected over a dozen tattoos. Some were self drawn like the happy faces he carved onto his knees to cheer himself up when he sat on the toilet, while others were the work of professionals.

Ozzy has a **red hooded ghoul** on his left pec and a **blue dragon with red flames** on the right side of his chest. On his left shoulder Ozzy has a **bat** and **wild witch's face**. He has both a **skull** with a **knife** through it and a **long pointed dagger** with an **'Ozzy'** banner on his left arm. He also has a **stick man figure** on his left wrist just below his thumb and a message across his left palm. The word **'THANKS'** is marked on his right palm.

Ozzy has a **rose** on his right shoulder with the word **'Sharon'** tattooed under it. On his right arm he has a full sleeve featuring his various **ghouls, demons, leaves** and **daggers**. Other tattoos include assorted occult symbols and a number **'3'** on his arm and a **sword** on his right thigh.

Ozzy's tattoos are as weird and wonderful as the man himself. But Ozzy explains them with typical candor: "When you're young, you're stupid. You do silly things. I did it (the **O-Z-Z-Y** tattoo across his knuckles) when I was 14. I was in jail for something. I could have had it removed, but why? It's my trademark. People stop me and say, 'Let me have a look at your hand.'"

P!nk

Born to humble roots in Doylestown, Pennsylvania, P!nk has carved a stellar career for herself as a multi-platinum selling, Grammy award winning R & B superstar and some time actress. She is also one of music's most recognizable fans of tattoo art and has been getting inked since she was thirteen years old.

She has over twenty tattoos – each one representing a significant event in her life. On the back of her neck she has a **barcode** with **'I 9879-II200-I 3'** which is a combination of her date of birth, favourite number and release date of her album *Mizzundastood*.

On her left shoulder she has a **guardian angel chasing a shooting star** while on her left arm she has a **swirling tribal design** and one half of a **broken heart** that says **'Best Friends'** (her best friend Laura Jeanne Wilson wears the other half). She also has memorial tattoos for her dogs **'Elvis'** and **'Sir Corky Moore'**. On her left wrist, she has a **razor blade** with the word **'Insecurity'** and a **small red star** which is shared by her producer Linda Perry.

On her right arm is a **'help button'** as well as several messages: **'Tru Luv'** (her former husband cyclist Carey Hart has a matching tattoo) and **'What Goes Around Comes Around'** in fancy script.

On her bikini line P!nk has a **red heart** with the **kanji** symbol for love but she saves her most famous tattoos for her legs. A huge **tribal dragon** on her left leg and matching **pink bows** on the back of her thighs. On her ankles P!nk has more kanji symbols for **luck, happiness** and **eternity** and her father and brother's **army dog tags**. There is also a **frog** on her left foot and a **heart** on each big toe.

P!nk says of her tattoos: "I think they are very incredibly sexy. I don't regret any of mine because they all represent a chapter in my life and that's what tattoos are for."

Brad Pitt

Brad Pitt once said that "heartthrobs are a dime a dozen" but since his sizzling debut as hitchhiking grifter in *Thelma and Louise*, he has consistently held his place in the Hollywood elite. Considered by many film fans to be one of the most attractive men alive, this actor, film producer, and social activist has won both a Golden Globe Award and an Academy Award as well as the hearts of Gwyneth Paltrow, Jennifer Aniston and latterly Angelina Jolie, with whom he has started a large family. Until recently Brad had shown little interest in tattoo art but it seems that his relationship with Angelina has opened his eyes to the joys of the needle. Nowadays Brad is as likely to be collecting tats as the couple is to be collecting children.

Brad's tattoos reflect a good deal about his nature. They display the cool understatement of a man who has little left to prove while revealing unexpected depths. He has a tattoo of a piece of **Arabic script** on the left side of his lower back which is believed to be **a prayer for his children**. On the underside of his left forearm, he has an enigmatic outline of **Oetzi, the Iceman**, and under this he has a line of words in French reading **'Absurdites de l' existence'**, which translates as **'life is absurd'**.

Most recently Brad has added an additional tribute to his partner when he had Angelina Jolie's birth date **(6/4/75)** inked on his stomach in Khmer, the ancient language of Cambodia.

Tattoo fans might be disappointed to know that the fuller covering of old school tattoos that Brad displayed in the movies such as *Ocean's Eleven* and particularly *Snatch* were fakes specially created for the role.

Prison Break

Prison Break is a Golden Globe and Emmy award-nominated TV show that tells the story of one man's ingenious plan to save his brother from execution by breaking them both out from the fictional Fox River Penitentiary.

Lincoln Burrows is on death row for the murder of the vice president's brother and only his brother Michael believes in his innocence. Frustrated by the legal system, Michael (who also happens to be the engineer who helped re-model the prison he has been sent to) takes part in an armed robbery in order to get incarcerated with his brother; but not before having himself tattooed with an elaborate design that contains all the hidden information the pair need to escape.

Michael tattoos his chest, back and both arms with a gothic fantasy of **angels** and **demons**. The artwork is monochrome with lots of thin lines and filled out with shading all of which is used to conceal vital information. The large **demon** on Michael's chest hides a map of the prison's underground network. While continuing the heaven and hell allegory his **angel** back piece shows a view of the prison from the air. The sleeves of the tattoo shirt are also covered with **formulas, names** and **codes** necessary to the escape hidden in dozens of **scrolls, bottles, playing cards** and other common tattoo imagery.

The tattoo featured on the show was designed by a real life tattoo artist, Tom Berg. Berg was also the artist who created Ralph Fiennes' tattoos for his role as a psychopath in the movie *Red Dragon*.

However Wentworth Miller, the actor who plays Michael, was not enough of a method actor to have the body suit done for real; his tattoos are fake. According to Wentworth, the process of applying the fake tats took two makeup artists between four and five hours to complete. Created by the same effects company that made Vin Diesel's tattoos for his role as Xander Cage in extreme sports smash "xXx", the designs featured in *Prison Break* are composed from a series of complex transfers that were glued onto the actor's skin. The designs were touched up by hand before being sealed with a flexible membrane.

The process allowed the actor to move around freely without disturbing the designs even when acting in physical or action scenes or coming into contact with water. After shooting, the tattoo was removed not by laser but with special make up solvents.

Christina Ricci

Christina Ricci has effortlessly made the difficult transition from child star to teen idol to respected actress. After first achieving fame in her role as Wednesday Addams in *The Addams Family*, the Emmy nominated actress made her name with a series of off beat cult roles in *The Ice Storm* and *Monster* as well as bigger budget fare like *Casper* and Tim Burton's *Sleepy Hollow*.

Always a complex character, Christina has been vocal about her difficult past and her triumph over a troubled upbringing that has found expression in some of her tattoos. One of her earliest and most prominent pieces is a representation of **Aslan**, the lion ruler of Narnia on her right shoulder. Christina has said that the tattoo is there to remind her of her childhood: "It's Aslan, the lion from *The Lion, The Witch And The Wardrobe*. It's a symbol of my hellish childhood. I struggled through my oppressive teenage years and when I turned 18 I escaped. Like Aslan I was finally free."

Along with Aslan, Christina has a **fairy** on the inside of her right wrist and a set of **praying hands** on her left hip though this tattoo has been modified and was originally a **bat**. She had a **bouquet of sweet peas** tattooed in the small of her back and the words **'Move or Bleed'** in fancy script on the left side of her ribcage. The name **'Jack'** was added on her right thigh in memory of one of her dogs. There is also a **mermaid** on her left ankle.

However her most striking addition is an old school **blue sparrow** in flight on her right breast. The New Orleans artist who added the bird commented that the actress had near perfect breasts. It's not clear if Christina was motivated by the flattery or their excellent work with the needle but she went on to tip her $150 for the $150 tattoo.

Nicole Richie

Reality TV star and singer Nicole Richie is the adopted daughter of Commodores singer Lionel Richie. Despite her recent drug problems, high profile run-ins with the law, and accusations of anorexia, she is perhaps best known for the three seasons she has starred alongside childhood friend Paris Hilton in smash TV series *The Simple Life*.

Most recently this bad girl has showed signs of settling down. She has a child with Good Charlotte guitarist and fellow tattoo enthusiast Joel Madden and the pair have also launched The Richie Madden Children's Foundation to raise money for mothers and their families in need. Nicole's most famous tattoo is the **rosary beads** that encircle her ankle ending with an ornate **cross** on the top of her foot. The religious influences in her life are also demonstrated by the **angel wings** found on her shoulder blades and a further **cross** on her lower back.

On the back of her neck, Nicole has **'Richie'** in old English font and a **red bow and ribbon**. She also has a **tiara** located on her hip and a set of **ballerina's slippers** in reference to a song her father wrote for her.

On the inside of her right wrist, Nicole has **a red shooting star**, a design that is also inked on two of her best friends, Quincy Jones' daughter Kidada and the late singer Aaliyah. On her left wrist, she has the word **'Virgin'** which she added in reference to her star sign – Virgo.

Famously Nicole also has a **'half'** tattoo of dots on her finger which was inked by mistake. The dots were added by Nicole herself when she was playing with the tattoo gun during a visit to a friend's tattoo parlor.

Dennis Rodman

Dennis Rodman is truly a larger than life character. The 6'7" former basketball player is best known for his defensive and rebounding ability, winning five NBA Championships with the Detroit Pistons and the Chicago Bulls. Since retiring from professional sport he has turned his hand to acting, music, wrestling and almost inevitably reality television with *Dennis Rodman's World Tour*.

Thanks to several tell-all biographies and many TV appearances, Rodman has become infamous for his eccentric behavior, bad language, dyed hair, piercings and tattoos rather than his considerable achievements as an athlete. He has also been linked to a series of high profile female celebrities including Carmen Electra and Madonna.

Dennis probably has too many tattoos to list. Most notable however are the powerful `tribal designs` he has in a necklace around his shoulders and the `twin bulls` he has mirrored on his chest.

"The worm" has full sleeves on both arms. On his right he has `'Mi Vida loca'` meaning `'my crazy life'` in fancy script on his shoulder above a `cross covered in vines` and a `naked devil woman` next to a `Harley Davidson`. On his left he has a `large red dice`, a `dolphin` and a `lucky horse shoe.` He also has a `tribal design` around his wrist which extends onto the back of his hand.

On his belly Dennis has a `nautical star` above an `Ankh`, the key of life, which surrounds his navel flanked by his initials `'D'` and `'R'` in gothic script.

But Dennis' tattoos just go to add another dimension to the growing legend. As his former coach Bob Hill once said of Rodman: "Beyond the hair, tattoos and earrings, he's just like you and me."

Henry Rollins

Musician Henry Rollins was born as plain Henry Lawrence Garfield. His parents' early divorce left him with a legacy of serious self esteem and anger issues which he initially diverted into books and later into weightlifting and punk rock. It was as a teenager that the reclusive Garfield began to transform himself into the muscle bound "Rollins" by discipline and sheer force of will.

Rollins' break came when he fronted the Californian hardcore punk band Black Flag throughout the Eighties. Following the band's break-up, he established his own record label and publishing company, 2.13.61 (named after his birthday), to release his own spoken word albums and the music of a new group, The Rollins Band. Rollins is now a respected singer and songwriter, spoken word artist, author, actor, publisher and broadcaster. Moreover he is instantly recognizable for the many rough and ready tattoos that cover his body.

His first tattoo was the **Black Flag logo** which he had tattooed on his left bicep aged 20 and which he later said was "the only one I every really needed." Over the years, he has added many more iconic images. He has a thick **bar code** on the back of his neck and also a matching **set of bars** tattooed in two places on his arms. His arms also feature a **coiled striped serpent** and a **Misfits skull**. There is also a large **black widow spider** on his shoulder.

Across his back, Rollins has a hugely intimidating full back piece of a **rising sun** beneath the words **'Search and Destroy'**. He also has a series of heartfelt messages such as **'Life is pain'** above **two skull masks** on his arm amid the various Celtic symbols, human faces and crests.

Some of Rollins' tattoos display great strength while others are timeless memories of his fears and weaknesses. As Rollins himself has said: "For me, tattooing was a way to not look like my Dad. Now they're just like freckles."

Sailor Jerry

When many of us think of "old school" tattoos, the chances are we will imagine designs created or inspired by Sailor Jerry. Ribald, humorous, brightly colored and nautically inspired, the Sailor Jerry style is immediately recognizable in the body art that adorns stars such as Amy Winehouse and Ewan Macgregor.

Norman "Sailor Jerry" Collins was indeed a sailor before he took up the needle. At the age of 19, he enlisted in the US Navy and traveled the world. It was while he was in the navy that he got his first tattoos and visited South East Asia. The trip exposed him to the art and imagery of the Orient which provided the inspiration for his creativity, indeed he would remain in correspondence with many of the Japanese tattoo masters he met throughout his life.

He opened his first business in Honolulu's Chinatown. At the time Honolulu was the only place on Hawaii where tattoo studios were located, being conveniently close to the docks that provided a constant stream of eager (and often drunken) sailors keen to commemorate their visit to the island with body art.

Competition was fierce among Honolulu's tattooists not least because the clientele largely had little time for nuance, meticulous attention to detail, and artistry (although Sailor Jerry excelled at all three; indeed it is claimed that his attention to detail was such that even the rigging in his nautical tattoos was accurate). Instead they were looking for bold, breath-taking designs which made the kind of statement that was worth peeling off your shirt to show off when you got home.

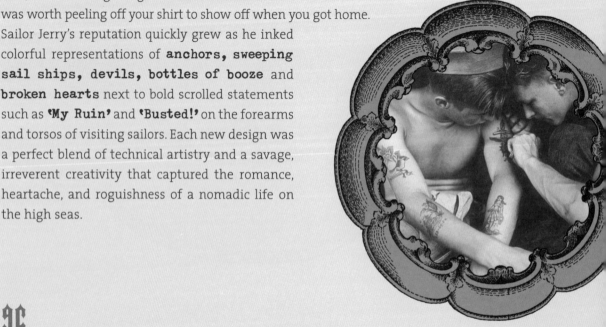

Sailor Jerry's reputation quickly grew as he inked colorful representations of **anchors, sweeping sail ships, devils, bottles of booze** and **broken hearts** next to bold scrolled statements such as **'My Ruin'** and **'Busted!'** on the forearms and torsos of visiting sailors. Each new design was a perfect blend of technical artistry and a savage, irreverent creativity that captured the romance, heartache, and roguishness of a nomadic life on the high seas.

No sailor's shore leave would be the same without the women he left behind, and Sailor Jerry will primarily be remembered for those he created. Already a key element of naval tattooing, Sailor Jerry's buxom, heart-breaking **maidens** with their long lashes and even longer legs stood out among his rivals' flash sheets for their sexiness, strength, and their allure of mystery.

But Sailor Jerry did a great deal more than carve out a reputation as one of the most innovative tattoo artists of his generation, he also instigated many of the technical advances in the art which are now commonplace.

He expanded the array of colors available to tattoo artists by developing his own pigments and created revolutionary needle formations which allowed him to ink his clients with reduced damage to their skin. His saloon was also one of the first to introduce the rigorous hygiene procedures we take for granted today, such as using needles only once and medical sterilization. Throughout his life he remained a staunch critic of the sloppy or poor quality tattooists that he referred to as "scab merchants."

With his grey hair and his pipe the Sailor Jerry his customers encountered as they sat in his studio chair might have seemed innocuous. However he regarded his tattoos as the ultimate rebellion against "the Squares". His work explored the essential weakness of human nature and the dark forces in the world that shape men and women.

Today the name of "Sailor Jerry" has come to represent an entire school of tattooing and his legacy lives on. His original designs and letters form the basis of a multi-million dollar business, Sailor Jerry, Ltd., which produces clothing, gifts and its own brand of rum; the very drink Sailor Jerry had inked on the arms of so many satisfied customers.

Nikki Sixx

When it comes to setting the baseline for rock and roll decadence you need look no further than Nikki Sixx. Throughout the Eighties he and his band Motley Crue blazed through the rock scene pushing the sex, drugs, and rock 'n' roll lifestyle to its limits. Sixx, the band's bass player and primary songwriter, has since become a recognized author and photographer.

Wild though he was Nikki will also be remembered for the women he married – both **Playboy** Playmates (Brandi Brandt and Baywatch star Donna D'Errico) – and his love of tattoo art.

Nikki is well on his way to a full body suit. In fact he has so many tattoos that even some of his more well known works are now covered by new designs. For example an old school **bleeding rose** on Nikki's chest has given way to a huge amount of Japanese influenced work. He has two deep red shoulder pieces that culminate at a **kanji** in the centre of his chest.

Nikki does however have a new flower, an **orchid** on his leg above his son's name, **Storm**. His son Decker features on his other leg with a large **tottenkopf**. His former wife, **Donna**, gets a mention in gothic script on the back of his neck and in the **rosary** designs they share on their feet.

The shoulder pieces form a seamless link to Nikki's sleeves which contain **playing cards**, **cherubs**, **dragons**, **flowers** and a **samurai face,** while across his back Nikki has a striking **sun design with a face** at the centre above a **dramatic battle** between an **angel** and a **devil**.

Nikki also shares a **Motley Crue** tattoo on his left shoulder with his band mates. He has the word **'SIXX'** and the number **'1958'** (the year of his birth) tattooed on his knuckles.

It seems kind of inevitable that Nikki would one day combine his love of women with tattoos and recently he has been begun a relationship with Miami Ink tattoo artist Kat Von D.

Britney Spears

It is well known that singer and actress-turned-tabloid obsession, Britney Spears, has a host of tattoos across her body. Unfortunately not all of these have been inked under the happiest of circumstances. Indeed the multi-platinum-selling star's history with the needle has been as unpredictable as her well-documented life.

In 2004 the *Toxic* star had a Kaballah healing symbol of three Hebrew characters inked on the back of her neck. The tattoo read **'mem,' 'hey'** and **'shin'** and referred to the wearer's ability to heal themselves. However three years later Britney decided to get the words removed by laser treatment.

"When she got the tattoo, Britney was in control of her life and her career. The whole world can see she's lost control, and the tattoo made her feel like a hypocrite," said a friend. Likewise she has recently had changes made to a pair of **pink dice** she had added to her inside left wrist to match those worn by former husband Kevin Federline.

During a recent meltdown in which Britney shaved her head, the troubled singer had a further two ill-advised tattoos added, a set of **red and pink lips** on her wrist, and a **black, white and pink cross** on her lower hip. These irresponsible additions by an unnamed tattoo artist drew universal condemnation from the tattoo community.

However Britney's other tattoos do represent better times in the star's life. On her lower back Britney has a cute **fairy** tattoo to show her child-like imagination; while on her stomach is a **flower** with the **Chinese symbol for mystery** in the middle. There are more **flowers** on her feet with a small **daisy** circling the second toe on her right foot and a **butterfly** leaving a vine on her left foot – all images of growth and rebirth.

The small **star** on Britney's right hand is meant to symbolize protection – it wouldn't be hard to argue that Ms Spears needs it more than most.

Spiritual
- What do they mean?

Angels & cherubs - Angels are meant to protect the wearer on earth and intercede on their behalf in heaven. They are often beautiful in their adult form or cute and youthful as cherubs. As opposites play a key part in tattoo tradition, they are often inked with devils.

Ankh - The key of life is an ancient Egyptian hieroglyph associated with Imhotep, the chief physician for the Pharaoh's family, who later became the god of medicine and healing.

Celtic cross - Known as the Wheel Cross or the Ring Cross, it is a Christian symbol from the Middle Ages which borrowed heavily from the pagan tradition. In Pagan lore, the cross represented the "plus sign" of male fertility combined with the circle of the female.

Devil - Satan features large in tattoo art, sometimes as a cuddly red wicked cartoon or as a grotesque monster with horns and cloven hooves. The tattoo is largely associated with resisting temptation.

Eye of Horus - In ancient Egypt, the Eye of Horus was a powerful symbol of protection. The eye of the falcon god is also meant to ensure good health.

Hand of Fatima - Fatima was the Prophet Muhammad's favourite daughter. Her hand is known in the Islamic world to avert the Evil Eye and hence act as a sign of good luck.

Sacred heart - A popular image in tattoo mythology as well as Roman Catholicism, the sacred heart represents the wounded heart of Jesus and the suffering of mankind.

Thunderbird - This mythical bird from North America has huge and terrible powers over natural elements, notably rainstorms. Often found on totem poles and in tribal tattoos, it connects the wearer with their ancestors and the life giving power of the elements.

Wicca symbols - Wicca is an Old English religion largely regarded as a combination of witchcraft and nature worship. Pentagrams, crescent moons and circles feature to evoke the power of the Goddess.

Virgin Mary - The Catholic symbol of love, patience and intercession, Mary is the ultimate guardian angel. She is usually portrayed in the traditional style, humble and in prayer covered by a blue veil and surrounded by a glorious halo.

Yin and Yang - This ancient Chinese symbol represents the duality of the cosmos. "Yin" (the black) and "yang" (the white) represent two sides of a valley bisected by shadow and sunlight; however it has also come to mean the pairing of male and female, positive and negative, and heaven and earth.

Suicide Girls

While celebrities may be the most high profile evangelists of the joys of body art, it is worth remembering that the world of tattoos is open to anyone who wishes to make a creative statement with their body. Suicide girls are a prime example of "ordinary" people who express their lives and interests in an extraordinary way. The term "suicide girls" refers to a sexy, sassy sub-culture of young women worldwide who are devotees of a unique, alternative culture that expresses itself through music, literature, sexuality, hair dye, make up, piercing, and tattooing. They have found a home on a hugely popular website of the same name, which features stylized pin-up photos and profiles submitted by the girls themselves.

Though the term "suicide girl" was first used by Fight Club author, Chuck Palahniuk, in his novel *Survivor*, the website's founders, Sean Suhl ("Sean") and Selena Mooney ("Missy Suicide"), adopted the name "suicide girls" to describe the sexually empowered, intelligent, and radical young women that they saw around them. As Mooney explains: "Suicide girls is a term my friends and I had been using to describe the girls we saw in Portland's Pioneer Square with skateboards in one hand, wearing a Minor Threat hoodie, listening to Ice Cube on their iPods while reading a book of Nick Cave's poetry. They are girls who didn't fit into any conventional sub-culture and didn't define themselves based on musical taste like punk, metal, goth, etc..." Mooney has suggested that the girls had also effectively committed "social suicide" by refusing to conform to the mainstream.

The Suicidegirls website functions not just as a photo gallery of fantastic tattoos but as a subscription based online community with message boards, blogs and interviews with key figures from both the popular and underground media.

Though the website was started in a tiny Portland loft apartment five years ago the founders have compared its impact to that of *Playboy* Magazine, which became both a "beacon and a guide" for an entirely new lifestyle. The website now attracts an audience of over 5 million visitors a month from dozens of countries. Nearly two thousand models have uploaded their pictures and the site has spawned a success-ful book, a DVD, a burlesque show and a clothing line. Celebrity fans include Dave Navarro, Courtney Love, *Star Trek*'s Wil Wheaton and Scott Ian of Anthrax.

Symbols

– What do they mean?

Anchor – The wearer of the anchor is likely to be a sailor, often with a military or naval background. Traditionally the anchor showed that a seaman had sailed the Atlantic Ocean however the anchor was also used by early Christians due to its resemblance to a cross.

Biohazard – This post-modern addition to the tattoo canon is popular for its intricate and geometric pattern, which is almost tribal. Recognized world-wide as a warning of a biological substance that is dangerous to humans, it also carries a tongue in cheek sub-context.

Cards and dice – Representing chance, cards and dice are used as talismans for good and bad luck. They might symbolize a lucky number or a traditional good hand like three sevens, or a royal flush, or a pair of dice showing a winning craps hand of two (snake eyes).

Dreamcatcher – Native American Indian legends tell of a Spider Woman who wove protective webs across the cradles of their children but as the tribes migrated to distant lands, mothers took to creating dreamcatchers to take on the task.

Hannya Mask – This scary mask is used in traditional Japanese "Noh" theatre; specifically to represent a jealous woman whose anger has so consumed her that she has become a demon.

Horseshoe – Horseshoes are best known as a lucky charm or amulet in the West but the Romans believed that its "U" shape could ward off evil. The shape has also been associated with a crescent moon and hence fertility.

Kanji characters – Kanji characters are the oldest of Japan's three writing systems. Kanji are ideograms – like Egyptian hieroglyphs – where a single symbol can represent an entire concept, such as beauty or contentment.

Nautical star – Based around Polaris, the North Star, a key reference point in maritime navigation. The nautical star symbolizes safe return home and good luck.

Rope – A traditional sailor's tattoo, seamen and dockhands often had a rope tattooed around their wrists to show their profession and their strength.

Skulls – Not surprisingly a skull often represents death. The skull and crossbones are also associated with piracy, again largely meaning death, and Davy Jones' Locker, the final resting place of drowned sailors.

Sailing ship – A fully rigged sailing ship can be quite a piece of art, for sailors they are used to indicate the wearer had successfully completed the dangerous journey around Cape Horn. Nowadays they show a fascination with a bygone age and the tattoo tradition.

Billy Bob Thornton

Billy Bob Thornton is an Oscar-winning screenwriter, actor and and singer. He came to fame starring in the film *Sling Blade*, and has since established himself as a versatile character actor in movies such as *Pushing Tin* and *Bad Santa*. He has also achieved a degree of notoriety for his Southern charm and many marriages, including several wildly eccentric and highly publicized years with the actress Angelina Jolie.

Billy Bob's first tattoo was a **heart** on his right forearm bearing his own name. His next tattoo was another **heart**, this time on his bicep, pierced by an arrow and reading **'Nothin' Doin'** (the name of his first band). Other band tattoos include an Allman Brothers **magic mushroom** on his calf. Also on his left arm he has a **rose** tattoo that he "got for a Mexican girl" and his star sign, **Leo**.

On his left arm he has a **lotus** with a blue pearl centre, a tribal **Celtic cross** and an ancient Buddhist symbol, the **ohm**. But perhaps Billy Bob's most fanciful piece of work is an **angel** that sits on the crook of his left arm. The tattoo covers the name of his ex wife **'Angelina.'** (Jolie). Beneath the angel is the word **'peace'**, which Billy Bob says is "basically, my way of saying, 'No hard feelings.'"

On Billy Bob's back he has three large pieces of work. He has a picture of the flag that flew in San Jacinto at the time of the fall of **the Alamo**, which he and several cast members all got after shooting a film about the epic event and inscribed with phrase **'Remember the Alamo'**. Along his spine in Art Deco script Billy Bob has **'Constance'** in tribute to the mother of his daughter, Connie Angland. Finally he has the names of his sons, **Willie, Harry,** and **Maddox,** interwoven with his name and Angelina's in the shape of an eagle in flight which, while being his favourite piece of work, was, according to Billy Bob, the most painful tattoo he's ever had done.

Justin Tim
Justin Timberl

Justin
Timberlake

Justin Timberlake, like Christina Aguilera and his ex girlfriend Britney Spears, is a former Mouseketeer who has achieved pop mega stardom and caught the body art bug.

Justin has had five separate pieces of work done since hitting the big time with boy band N'Synch though, according to rumor, his mother has told him he's not allowed to get any more. Justin explained, "I've got five and she thinks I'll regret it when I'm old if I have any more."

Justin hails from Memphis in the heart of America's Bible Belt; it was here where he first sang in the local Baptist church in which his father was choir director. So it's no surprise to find religious influences in many of his tattoos. He has a large **cross** on his upper arm. He also has an ornate **guardian angel** on his upper back, while the angel at the centre of his fancy back piece holds a **ribbon** which bears his mother's initials.

On Justin's upper calf he has an **astrological band** that wraps around the leg which displays Justin's birth sign – **Aquarius** – at it's centre.

Justin's other leg is devoted to music with a small Chinese symbol that represents music and song. Beneath the Chinese character is found an ankle band that forms a unique composite tribute to his N'Synch career. **Flames** were N'Synch's logo for their first album and the **red ropes** were associated with their final *Celebrity* album. Justin's N'Synch inspired tattoo is finished with the **marionette** on his ankle to represent the puppet theme of their *No Strings Attached* album.

Despite his mother's prohibition on further work, Justin got a taste of full body coverage when he was covered in temporary work for his role as a criminal in the 2006 movie *Alphadog*. Justin himself has promised that he will get just one more piece done – a tattoo to immortalize the name of the woman he finally marries.

Tribal style

Tribal tattoos have enjoyed a huge surge in popularity in recent years. Tribal style is typically composed of pointed and curved elements that are bold and eye-catching. Their mystery, symbolism and power have meant that such designs have found their way onto the skin of stars such as Robbie Williams, Tommy Lee, P!nk, and Dave Blaine.

Since the earliest days of mankind, tattoos have been used to decorate and enhance the skin of men and women. While some were simple decorations, they often marked a person as a member of a group, or religion, or celebrated the passing of a key event in their life. Our basic survival instincts have always led us to seek the protection of groups. It is for this reason that tribal tattoos retain their unique power in our society.

The discovery of the mummified remains of a Bronze Age man demonstrated that the popularity of tribal tattooing is far from a modern phenomenon. Oetzi the Ice Man had both his arms, his legs and his torso covered with elaborate designs of mythical creatures. Tattoos have also been found on Ice Age rock carvings of hunters and even Egyptian mummies. Indeed tattooing has been found to be widespread among the ancient people of the Philippines, Borneo, Africa, North America, South America, Europe, Japan, Cambodia, New Zealand, and China to name a few.

In Western culture, tribal tattooing was banned by early Christians, who believed that the body should not be marked as it belonged to God. However there has been a widespread resurgence of the tribal practice of tattooing in recent years and particularly in tribal designs that give the wearer a direct link to their forefathers.

Tribal tattoos are known to have served as a mark of status or symbol of religious devotion. They may indicate a person's bravery, attractiveness, or bring good luck. But it is unfair to say that they follow a particular style. Polynesian tattoos tend to be rounded and complex while much of Samoan tattooing is linear and geometric – it is also worth noting that Pacific Rim cultures are not known for their tattooed arm bands (an enduring staple of modern Western tribal body art.)

The creative possibilities of such tattooing are another key reason for their popularity. Tribal tattoos invariably feature unique artwork based upon pure black lines that wrap around the body, and leave the design open to several different meanings.

But some traditions may be best left in the past. Tribal cultures used to created tattoos by cutting designs into the skin and rubbing the resulting wound with ink or ashes; Maoris used scraping tools to create scarification; while others hand-tapped the ink into the skin using sharpened sticks or animal bones. In modern times, most of us may choose the safer, less painful electronic needle gun.

20th Century

– History part three

Since the 1960s tattoos have slowly taken their place in mainstream culture. As well as having many celebrity fans, today tattoos are experiencing a huge resurgence in popularity with people all around the world, particularly the US and Europe. A 2006 study by the Journal of the American Academy of Dermatology found that 24 per cent of Americans between 18 and 50 had at least one tattoo; probably inked in one of America's 20,000 tattoo parlors.

With growing demand has come an exponential rise in quality. In recent years the demand for unique and eye-catching designs has resulted in more and more talented artists choosing to forego careers in advertising or fine art to make a good living in the tattoo industry. Advances in tattoo pigments and increasingly sophisticated equipment has meant that the quality and longevity of the tattoos being created continues to improve.

Indeed the developments in the industry have meant that tattooing has also never been safer. A properly equipped, modern tattoo studio will use an inventory usually only found in hospitals to protect the health of their clients and employees; such as disposable gloves, antiseptic wipes, biohazard containers, and single use needles, as well as an autoclave to sterilize equipment. Customers can also expect their tattoo artists to give them useful advice on the aftercare of their tattoos when they leave their chair as well as its design and styling.

While the traditional "tattoo parlor" with all its seedy outlaw associations is still in existence, increasingly customers are making carefully researched decisions about the individual artists they choose to create their one of a kind designs.

Even tattoos themselves are changing thanks to advances in technology. Modern ink might contain pigments created from finely ground plastics such as Acrylonitrile butadiene styrene (ABS) which allow extremely vivid tattooing with clearer, longer-lasting lines that are largely resistant to the fading and blurring of traditional inks.

Even more radical are UV tattoos created with an ink that is completely invisible in normal daylight but which glows in bright lurid colors under ultra-violet light. Whether a person chooses to get tattooed to bond with their cultural heritage, commemorate a loved one, decorate their body, or simply because they like the idea of it, there has never been a better time to get inked.

Mark Wahlberg
Mark Wahlberg

Mark Wahlberg

After a troubled childhood which included drug abuse and time spent in jail, Mark Wahlberg first burst into the public eye not as an actor but as a rapper. He followed his older brother, the New Kids on the Block star Donnie Wahlberg, into the music business singing with the Funky Bunch. Immediately recognizable for his sculpted body and chiseled good looks "Marky Mark" soon shot to the top of the charts on both sides of the Atlantic with the rap anthem "Good Vibrations". He cemented his position as a sex symbol with a legendary advertising campaign for Calvin Klein.

From these unpromising beginnings, Mark went on to carve out a career as an Oscar-nominated actor, equally at home being directed in *The Departed* by Martin Scorsese as he was taking the lead in big budget sci fi epics like *Planet of the Apes*.

Several of Mark's tattoos find their roots in his Irish Catholic upbringing in Boston. He has the cartoon character **Sylvester the cat** with **Tweety** in his mouth on his left ankle, which in fact covers up an old **shamrock** tattoo. He also has a **rosary** around his neck which was created partly to justify his love of body art: "I was 12 years old and I got a homemade tattoo that I did myself with Indian ink. So then my parish priest said I was going to hell because I marked my body. So I decided to fill my body with religious tattoos."

The actor also has tattoos on his shoulders. A portrait of reggae legend Bob Marley tattoo with the words **'One Love'** on the left and **'Wahlberg'** superimposed on a graffiti style **'MW'** along with his birth date and his parents' initials on the right shoulder, though it's unclear whether his mother approved of the gesture. During an appearance on the David Letterman show, Mark revealed that he had promised his mother that the inked designs would "wear off in a couple of years."

Pharrell Williams

Pharrell Williams came to fame as one half of The Neptunes, one of hip hop's most successful production duos. Over the past decade, Pharrell and his partner Chad Hugo have mixed stripped down funk, off kilter percussion, and spacey effects to create the unique Neptunes sound, and along the way produced hits for artists like Kelis, Usher, Snoop Dogg, Britney Spears, and P Diddy.

Pharrell plays the drums, keyboard, and sings. It is with these skills that he has gone on to carve a niche for himself as a solo performer and a serial entrepreneur, scoring success as a singer, rapper, songwriter, skateboarder, and as the founder of the clothes line, Billionaire Boys Club. Add to these achievements his role as the lead singer and drummer of the funk-rock band, N*E*R*D and you will not be surprised to discover that he is thought to be one of hip hop's most wealthy entertainers; worth a cool $155 million.

Pharrell's tattoos are classy black line drawings with a few extra colors. They betray a classical influence and often draw on quasi-religious themes and renaissance art for inspiration.

On the back of his neck Pharrell has a **guardian angel** complete with **sword** and **shield**. On his left arm he has **two naked women** in a fetal position on his bicep and an ornate half sleeve on his forearm. The sleeve features **angels** once again, this time **two cherubs kissing** in a heavenly scene above the portrait of a **woman's face**.

On his right forearm he has a long **male angel** and above it a large ornate **abstract** design that covers his bicep and shoulder.

So how does Pharrell combine his religious tattoos are with the temptations of being one the world's most attractive and successful recordings artists? Pharrell explains that: "At the end of the day, the Lord knows I have no malice in my heart. But I've got tattoos, and I still fornicate."

Robbie Williams

After David Beckham, pop star Robbie Williams is probably the UK's most prominent exponent of the tattoo. Over the years he has added a whopping 14 designs, numbers and scripts to express his unique personality. Each one has a unique significance in the singer's life story and expresses his deep love for friends and family.

Robbie picked up his first tattoo while he was still with the boy band Take That. The **Celtic cross** inked on his right hip was meant to protect Robbie against the temptations of the superstar lifestyle.

Robbie has a striking **Maori** tattoo in a partial sleeve across his left shoulder. The tattoo tells the story of Robbie's life in a symbolic series of the sharp pointed spirals. On his right shoulder is the **face of a lion,** symbolizing masculinity and strength. Surrounding the lion are two pieces of word play typical of Robbie's cheeky sense of humor **'Born to be mild'** and **'Elvis, grant me serenity'**. Robbie calls a further tattoo under his right arm the "Christian" as it depicts the crucifixion. Robbie has several tattoos that deal with his life as a touring musician.

A pair of swallows on his belly is an "old school" maritime design traditionally meant to represent a safe return home from traveling and the sheet music from The Beatles song **'All You Need Is Love'** is on his lower back. In 2004 Robbie added a symbol from Ancient Egypt, the **Eye of Horus**, to his neck to protect him from evil spirits. While under his left arm, he has the coat of arms of his birthplace, Burslem, Stoke on Trent. Robbie has many word-based tattoos. Between his first and second right-hand knuckles, he has the word **'Love'**. On his right forearm he has the phrase **'I Love U'** in old English and on his left the word **'Mother'**.

The chain of letters around Robbie's neck reads **'chacun à son goût'**, which means "everyone has got his own taste". Despite being French, this tattoo was actually done in LA and, by Robbie's account, was so painful he had to stop to recover.

In tribute to his family, behind his ear is the letter **B** – the first letter of his grandmother's name (Betty). On his wrists are **'Jack'** and **'Farrell'**, his grandfather's name, along with a **small heart**. He also has the number **1023** on his left wrist, corresponding to **'J'** (the 10th letter of the alphabet) and **'W'** (the 23rd) respectively (the initials of his best friend, actor Jonathan Wilkes).

Amy Winehouse

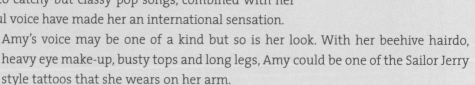

While Amy Winehouse's debut album *Frank* topped the charts in the Britain, it wasn't until the release of its follow-up, *Back to Black*, that she went into orbit world-wide, collecting five Grammys and two Ivor Novello Awards. Since then the "Rehab" star has spent so much time in the tabloid press that it's easy to forget she is a talented singer-songwriter whose skilful arrangements of soul, jazz and R&B into catchy but classy pop songs, combined with her distinctive soulful voice have made her an international sensation.

Amy's voice may be one of a kind but so is her look. With her beehive hairdo, heavy eye make-up, busty tops and long legs, Amy could be one of the Sailor Jerry style tattoos that she wears on her arm.

She got her first tattoo aged 15 and now has at least a dozen more. "I just wanted a Betty Boop on my bum," she explained. Now she has two **Betty Page style pin up girls** on her right arm (one with the word **'Cynthia'** next to her and the other holding a fan), a lightning bolt and a singing bird on her inside right forearm surrounded by the words **'Never clip my wings'**.

On her left shoulder she has **'Daddy's'** written in fancy script above a **lucky horseshoe** and a **large naked pin up girl** on her bicep. There is a **feather** which she had tattooed for strength on the inside of her left forearm.

Amy has a **winged ankh** between her shoulders and a **button pocket** over her heart with the word **'Blake's'** in reference to her husband, Blake Fielder-Civil. She also has an old school nautical **anchor** surrounded by **'Hello sailor'** on her belly.

It seems that Amy has no intention to stop adding tattoos to her body. Recently she warned: "I'm planning my most ambitious tattoo yet. You can never have enough tats."

Rob Zombie

He may look terrifying with his torn clothes, shaggy hair, and beard but hard rock singer turned filmmaker Rob Zombie is a multi-talented songwriter, producer, artist, and actor. He has sold nearly 25 million records as a solo artist and with his band White Zombie and scripted, produced, and directed the 2003 gore classic, *House of 1000 Corpses*.

Rob is also a forthright vegetarian and an accomplished artist. Not unsurprisingly he has many tattoos, all of which were designed by himself in association with the Chicago based tattoo artist Guy Aitchison. "I always liked the idea of them." Rob said. "The only reason I never got one before was that I never saw one that was really great until I saw Guy Aitchison's work. The last thing you want is a bad tattoo."

Mostly his body art features cartoonish horror-themed images and includes **skulls, devils,** and **movie monsters** from the Hollywood golden era. Most of his work to-date has been confined to his arms where Rob is quickly working towards two full sleeves. Key pieces include a **topless cowboy woman** with **smoking pistols** above a large **skull and cross bones** with its eyes popping on his right bicep and a **rampant female cyber warrior** above a spooky looking **devil mask** on his left. Further down his left arm he has another **topless woman** in flame red. While a great deal of thought goes into his creations, Rob still likes to keep his choice of pieces fairly free and easy: "I always come up with an idea at the last second and say to myself, 'Gee, I hope I like it tomorrow.'"

Not a man to be trifled with, Rob Zombie is someone who approaches his body art as he would other artistic projects and is prepared to accept bad choices as well as the good. Rob says of his attitude to tattooing "You want one, you get one. It hurts. You like it or you don't."

Index

Aaliyah 90

Aguilera, Christina 10-11, 110

Aitchison, Guy 125

American Indians 36, 59

anchors 70, 96, 106, 122

Anderson, Pamela 12-13, 62

angels & cherubs 17, 18, 20, 26, 67, 76, 82, 86, 90, 98, 102, 108, 110, 118

Angland, Connie 108

animals 14-15
   see also specific animals (eg bears)

Aniston, Jennifer 84

ankh 34, 92, 102, 122

armbands & bracelets 12, 17, 40, 42, 44, 59, 67, 70, 76, 78, 82, 92

Armstrong, Billie Joe 16-17

artworks 26, 78

Arvizu, "Fieldy" 74

Auf der Maur, Melisa 52

Balzary, Michael (Flea) 44-5

Banks, Sir Joseph 29

Barat, Carl 39

barcodes 82, 94

Barker, Travis 22-3

Barrymore, Drew 18-19

bats 78, 80, 88

bears 14, 28, 60

Beckham, David 20-1, 103, 120

Beckham, Victoria 20

Berg, Tom 86

Bertrand, Marcheline 56

biker tattoos 24-5, 52

biohazard 106

birds 14, 15, 44, 54, 62, 120, 122
   see also specific birds (eg bluebirds)

Blaine, David 26-7, 112

bluebirds 14

Bourdain, Anthony 74

bows & ribbons 82, 90, 110

Boy George 50-1

bracelets see armbands & bracelets

Brandt, Brandi 98

Brass, Darren 74

Bratman, Jordan 10

bulls 14, 92

Burns, Pete 34

butterflies 14, 18, 33, 34, 68, 100

Calzaghe, Joe 33

Cape Fear 30-1

carp 15, 54, 62

cars 17, 22

cartoon characters 60, 62, 68, 116, 122

Cates, Melanie Lynn 60

cats 14

Cave, Nick 104

Celtic crosses 33, 42, 102, 108, 120

Celtic tattoos 28, 32-3, 44, 59

Cher 34-5

cherry blossom 46, 48

cherubs see angels & cherubs

Chisholm, Melanie 59

chrysanthemums 34, 46

Churchill, Lady Randolph 70

Churchill, Sir Winston 70

claddagh 32

Clapp, Philip John (Johnny Knoxville) 60-1

clover, four-leaf 46, 67

Cobain, Kurt 67

Collins, Norman "Sailor Jerry" 96-7

Cook, Captain James 29, 70

Coppola, Sofia 59

criminals 25, 29, 30, 55

Cronenberg, David 25

crosses 18, 20, 30, 33, 34, 42, 50, 56, 70, 78, 90, 92, 100, 102, 108, 110, 120

Culkin, Macaulay 48

daggers 48, 80

daisies 46, 100

De Niro, Robert 30-1

Depp, Johnny 36-7

D'Errico, Donna 98

devils & demons 68, 80, 86, 92, 96, 98, 102, 125

dice 22, 68, 92, 100, 106

Diesel, Vin 86

dogs 82

Doherty, Pete 38-9

dolphins 14, 78, 92

dots 25, 90

doves 14

dragonflies 14, 48

dragons 32, 48, 54, 56, 62, 70, 80, 82, 98

dreamcatchers 106

eagles 25, 59, 62, 108

Edison, Thomas 71

Electra, Carmen 78, 92

elephants 44

Eminem 40-1

eye of Horus 102, 120

faces & portraits 17, 20, 26, 40, 44, 59, 60, 68, 80, 84, 98, 116, 118

fairies 76, 88, 100

Farrell, Colin 42-3

Fatima, hand of 102

Federline, Kevin 100

Fergusson, Craig 74

Fielder-Civil, Blake 122

Fiennes, Ralph 86

flags 22, 94, 108

flames 25, 110

Flea 44-5

flowers 10, 17, 18, 22, 34, 42, 46-7, 54, 62, 76, 88, 98, 100
   see also specific flowers (eg roses)

four-leaf clover 46, 67

frogs 82

Garfield, Henry Lawrence (Henry Rollins) 94-5

Garver, Chris 74

Gellar, Sarah Michelle 48-9

George V (King of England) 70

gothic symbols 68, 80

Green, Tom 18

Grohl, Dave 67

Hagen, Nina 59

Hamilton, James 74

hand of Fatima 102

Hannya mask 106

Harada, Yoji 74

Hart, Carey 82

Hart, Melissa Joan 48

hearts 22, 30, 34, 39, 48, 64, 67, 68, 76, 82, 96, 103, 108

Hendrix, Jimi 44

hikae 54

Hill, Bob 92

Hilton, Paris 90

history 28-9, 54-5, 70-1, 96-7, 112-13, 114-15

Homme, Josh 52-3

horseshoes 68, 92, 107, 122

Horus, eye of 102, 120

Hugo, Chad 118

Ian, Scott 105

initials see names & initials

irezumi 54, 55

ivy & vines 17, 18, 47, 67, 76, 92

James, Ami 74

Japanese-style tattoos 15, 17, 22, 25, 46, 54-5, 62, 70, 96, 98

jasmine 47

Jolie, Angelina 56-7, 84, 108

Jones, Kidada 90

Jones, Quincy 90

kanji characters 34, 54, 56, 78, 82, 98, 107

Kiedis, Anthony 58-9

kisses & lips 62, 100

Klum, Heidi 59

Knoxville, Johnny 60-1

koi 15, 54, 62

ladybirds 15
languages and alphabets other than English 10, 17, 20, 25, 42, 48, 56, 64, 76, 78, 84, 92, 100, 110, 120
Lee, Tommy 12, 13, 62-3, 112
Lemmy 52
Lennon, John 64
Letterman, David 116
Levi, Primo 26
lightning bolts 60, 122
lions 15, 88, 120
lips & kisses 62, 100
lizards 15
Locklear, Heather 62
logos 17, 22, 25, 40, 60, 78, 94, 98
Lohan, Lindsay 64-5
lotus flowers 50, 108
Love, Courtney 66-7, 105

MacDonald, John D 30
MacGregor, Ewan 96
Madden, Joel 90
Madonna 92
magic mushrooms 40, 108
Manson, Marilyn 68-9
Maori tattoos 29, 113, 120
maps 86
Margera, Bam 74
Mathers, Kim 40
Mayer, John 47
Memento 72-3
mermaids 39, 88
messages & quotations 10, 17, 20, 22, 25, 26, 30, 36, 39, 40, 42, 52, 56, 60, 62, 64, 72, 78, 82, 84, 88, 92, 94, 96, 108, 120, 122
Miami Ink 74-5
Milano, Alyssa 76-7
Miller, Jonny Lee 56
Miller, Wentworth 86,

87
Mitchum, Robert 30
Moakler, Shanna 22
Mooney, Selena 104
Moorish, Lisa 39
Moss, Kate 39
Muellerleile, Marianne 72
mushrooms, magic 40, 108
music 120

names & initials 10, 12, 17, 18, 20, 22, 30, 36, 39, 40, 42, 44, 50, 52, 56, 60, 62, 67, 78, 80, 88, 90, 92, 98, 100, 108, 110, 116, 120
Navarro, Dave 78-9, 105
Nolan, Christopher 72
Nolte, Nick 30
numbers 17, 20, 22, 26, 36, 40, 56, 72, 78, 80, 82, 84, 86, 98
Núñez, Chris 74

occult symbols 68, 80
O'Connell, Jerry 48
O'Connor, Sinéad 59
O'Reilly, Samuel 71
O'Riordan, Dolores 32
Oetzi the Iceman 84, 112
Osbourne, John Michael "Ozzy" 80-1
Osbourne, Sharon 67, 80
ouroboros 76

Palahniuk, Chuck 104
Paltrow, Gwyneth 84
panthers 30
Peaches 52
peacocks 15
Pearce, Guy 72, 73
Pennypacker, J Morgan 74
Perry, Linda 82
piercings 10, 62, 104
pigs 78

Pilkington, Ronnie 40
P!nk 82-3, 112
Pitt, Brad 56, 84-5
playing cards 22, 26, 52, 78, 86, 90, 106
portraits see faces & portraits
Prinze Jr, Freddie 48
Prison Break 86-7
prisoners 25, 30

quotations see messages &quotations

razors 52, 82
Reid, Tara 48
religious symbols 22, 30, 50, 54, 88, 103, 118, 120
see also specific symbols (eg crosses)
ribbons & bows 82, 90, 110
Ricci, Christina 88-9
Richie, Lionel 90
Richie, Nicole 90-1
Riley, Thomas 71
Rodman, Dennis 92-3
Rollins, Henry 94-5
ropes 107, 110
rosary beads 76, 90, 98, 116
roses 17, 40, 47, 78, 80, 98, 108
Ryder, Winona 36

Sailor Jerry 96-7, 122
sailors' tattoos 14, 29, 70, 96, 106, 107, 120
Schiffmacher, Hank 59
Scorsese, Martin 30, 116
Sgambati, Albert 68
shamrocks 46, 116
ships 96, 107
Sixx, Nikki 98-9
skulls 17, 22, 25, 36, 39, 68, 78, 80, 94, 107, 125
Skye, Ione 59

Slater, Mikey 74
snakes 15, 25, 28, 44, 59, 70, 76, 78, 94
South, Alfred Charles 71
sparrows 36, 88
Spears, Britney 100-1, 110, 118
spiders 94
Spinks, Leon 60
spiritual symbols 102-3
see also specific symbols (eg ankh)
star signs 90, 108, 110
stars 17, 18, 25, 50, 62, 64, 67, 82, 90, 92, 100, 107
Stringer, Donovan 68
Suhl, Sean 104
Suicide Girls 104-5
suns 94, 98
swifts 14
symbols 14-15, 32-3, 46-7, 102-3, 106-7
see also specific symbols (eg snakes)

Taylor, Jason 74
techniques and equipment 30, 55, 71, 72, 97, 113, 115
Thomas, Jeremy 18
Thornton, Billy Bob 56, 108-9
thunderbirds 44, 103
tigers 17, 54, 56, 59, 62
Timberlake, Justin 110-11
tree of life 33
tribal tattoos 12, 26, 29, 42, 50, 59, 60, 62, 82, 92, 112-13
triquetra 32
triskells 44

UV tattoos 115

Victoria (Queen of England) 70

vines see ivy & vines
Virgin Mary 22, 103
Voight, Jon 56
Von D, Kat 74, 75, 98

Wagner, Charlie 71
Wahlberg, Donnie 116
Wahlberg, Mark 116-17
Warner, Amelia 42
wedding bands 12, 42, 62
Wessman, Luke 74
Wheaton, Wil 105
wicca symbols 103
Williams, Pharrell 118-19
Williams, Robbie 112, 120-1
Wilson, Laura Jeanne 82
Winehouse, Amy 96, 122-3
wolves 15, 28
women 78, 97, 118, 122, 125
words see messages; names

Yakuza 25, 55
yin & yang 103

Zombie, Rob 124-5

Acknowledgements

Alamy/plainpicture GmbH & Co. KG 102; /Chris Willson 54.
Capital Pictures/Phil Loftus 35.
Corbis/Mario Anzuoni/Reuters 45; /Arctic-Images 114; /Tibor Bozi 94, 95; /Stephane Cardinale/People Avenue 3, 10; /Stephane Cardinale/Eric Robert/Sygma 109; /Markus Cuff 113; /Henry Diltz 44; /Rune Hellestad 40; /The Mariners' Museum 97; /Jessica Miller 79; /Steven C. Mitchell/epa 123; /Tony Mott/S.I.N. 81; /Gianni Dagli Orti 28; /Darren Staples/Reuters 20; /Shannon Stapleton/Reuters 115; /Stonehill/zefa 71; /Frank Trapper 18, 66.
Famous 16, 111.
Getty Images 29; /Brian Ach/WireImage 90; /Bryan Bedder 57; /Robert Bertoia 61; /Gareth Cattermole 38; /Michael Caulfield/WireImage 91; /Shawn Ehlers/WireImage 65; /Shirlaine Forrest/WireImage 39; /Jon Furniss/WireImage 19, 49; /Steve Granitz/WireImage 43; /Mike Guastella/WireImage 4, 78; /Frazer Harrison 85; /John M. Heller 98; /Dave Hogan 50, 51; /Mark Von Holden/WireImage 14; /Chris Jackson 36; /Simone Joyner 122; /Donald Kravitz 41; /Jeff Kravitz/ FilmMagic 13, 101; /Jean Baptiste Lacroix/WireImage 48; /David Livingston 75; /Mark Mainz 120; /Jeffrey Mayer/ WireImage 76, 77; /David McNew 107; /MPI 96; /Kazuhiro Nogi/AFP 55; /Ralph Notaro 74; /Scott Olson 24; /John Parra/ WireImage 99; /Chris Polk/FilmMagic 23; /Popperfoto 70; /Jason Squires/WireImage 11; /STR/AFP 9, 15; /David Teuma 17; /Noel Vasquez 21; /Theo Wargo/WireImage 89; /Kevin Winter 124; /Scott Wintrow 27, 93; /Jonathon Wood 121
The Kobal Collection/Summit Entertainment 73; /Universal 31.
PA Photos/Mark Cuthbert/UK Press 106; /David Davies/PA Wire 33; /Matt Sayles/AP 37.
PR Photos/Glenn Harris 105.
Reuters/Jim Ruymen 68.
Rex Features 2, 6, 58, 103, 119, 69; /c.20thC.Fox/Everett 87; /Brian Appio/Vistalux 53; /David Buchan 117; /Humberto Carreno 47; 84; Peter Carrette 62; /Huw John 83; /KPA/Zuma 104; /Andy Paradise 63; /Sipa Press 32; /Debra L. Rothenberg 82; /Jim Smeal/BEI 64; /Richard Young 118.
Shutterstock/iofoto 46.

How to apply temporary tattoos

WARNING: do not put on sensitive skin as the adhesive can cause allergic reactions.

1. Clean and dry the area of your skin you want to tattoo.

2. Cut out the chosen tattoo and remove the transparent film.

3. Place the tattoo face down onto the skin.

4. Wet the tattoo completely and gently rub with a damp cloth or sponge.

5. Peel the corner of the tattoo gently to check if it has transferred, if not, press down and wet again.

Your tattoos can last for several days if transferred carefully.

Temporary Tattoos inspired by 1 Ashlee Simpson 2 Amy Winehouse 3 Lindsay Lohan 4 Dave Navarro 5 Angelina Jolie 6 Johnny Depp 7 Pete Doherty 8 Pamela Anderson 9 Nicole Richie 10 Victoria Beckham 11 Justin Timberlake 12 Kate Moss 13 David Beckham 14 Britney Spears 15 Christina Aguilera 16 Ozzy Osbourne